First World War
and Army of Occupation
War Diary
France, Belgium and Germany

27 DIVISION
Divisional Troops
Royal Army Medical Corps
82 Field Ambulance
21 December 1914 - 30 November 1915

WO95/2259/2

The Naval & Military Press Ltd
www.nmarchive.com
Published in association with The National Archives

Published by

The Naval & Military Press Ltd

Unit 10 Ridgewood Industrial Park,
Uckfield, East Sussex,
TN22 5QE England
Tel: +44 (0) 1825 749494

www.naval-military-press.com

www.nmarchive.com

This diary has been reprinted in facsimile from the original. Any imperfections are inevitably reproduced and the quality may fall short of modern type and cartographic standards.

© Crown Copyright
Images reproduced by permission of The National Archives, London, England, 2015.

Contents

Document type	Place/Title	Date From	Date To
Heading	WO95/2259/2		
Heading	27th Division Medical 82nd Field Ambulance Dec 1914-Nov 1915		
Heading	121/4611 27th Division No. 82 Field Ambulance Vol I		
War Diary	Winchester	21/12/1914	21/12/1914
War Diary	Southampton	21/12/1914	21/12/1914
War Diary	Havre	22/12/1914	24/12/1914
War Diary	Auque	25/12/1914	31/12/1914
Heading	Jan 1915 Feb 1915 82nd Field Ambulance-27th Division Vol I		
War Diary	Arcques	01/01/1915	07/01/1915
War Diary	Caistre	07/01/1915	08/01/1915
War Diary	Boeschepe	09/01/1915	27/02/1915
Heading	121/5256 March 1915 82nd Field Ambulance-27th Division Vol II		
War Diary	Boeschepe	01/03/1915	31/03/1915
Heading	121/5408 April 1915 82nd Field Ambulance Vol III		
War Diary	Boeschepe	02/04/1915	04/04/1915
War Diary	Ypres	04/04/1915	14/04/1915
War Diary	Vlamertinge G.11.a	15/04/1915	28/04/1915
War Diary	Farm G.11.a	29/04/1915	30/04/1915
Heading	27th Division 82nd Field Ambulance Vol IV May 1915		
War Diary	Farm G.11.a	02/05/1915	04/05/1915
War Diary	Poperinghe	06/05/1915	28/05/1915
War Diary	Armentieres	29/05/1915	30/06/1915
Heading	27th Division 82nd Field Ambulance Vol V From 1st To 31st July 1915		
War Diary	Armentieres	01/07/1915	15/07/1915
War Diary	Ferme Rosiere (Waterlands) Sheet 36: B.26.b.6.8	16/07/1915	18/07/1915
War Diary	Ferme Rosiere	19/07/1915	31/07/1915
Heading	27th Division 82nd Field Ambulance Vol VI From 1-31.8.15 August 1915		
War Diary	Ferme Rosiere	01/08/1915	31/08/1915
Miscellaneous	Appendix I Medical Arrangements For 82 Infantry Brigade	29/08/1915	29/08/1915
Heading	27th Division 82nd Field Ambulance Vol VII Sept. 15		
War Diary	Ferme Rosiere	01/09/1915	05/09/1915
War Diary	L'Estrade	05/09/1915	15/09/1915
War Diary	Ferme Molleghem Petit Sec Bois	16/09/1915	20/09/1915
War Diary	Morcourt	21/09/1915	21/09/1915
War Diary	Chignolles	21/09/1915	25/09/1915
War Diary	Proyart	25/09/1915	30/09/1915
Heading	27th Division 82nd Field Ambulance Oct. 1915 Vol VIII		
War Diary	Proyart	01/10/1915	24/10/1915
War Diary	On The March	25/10/1915	26/10/1915
War Diary	Fresnoy	26/10/1915	31/10/1915
Heading	27th Div Portion of a War Diary Fardl 30.11.15 82nd Fd. Amb. 11-14 Oct 1915 Vol VIII		
Heading	27th Div F/177/1 Nov 1915 82nd Fd Amb. Nov Vol IX		

War Diary	Fresnoy-Au-Val	01/11/1915	05/11/1915
War Diary	Fresnoy	05/11/1915	26/11/1915
War Diary	H.M.T. Saturnia	26/11/1915	30/11/1915

WO 95/2259/2

27TH DIVISION
MEDICAL

82ND FIELD AMBULANCE
DEC 1914 - NOV 1915

121/4611
24th Division

No. 82 Field Ambulance
Vol I

Dec 1914

Army Form C. 2118.

WAR DIARY
or
INTELLIGENCE SUMMARY
(Erase heading not required.)

Instructions regarding War Diaries and Intelligence Summaries are contained in F. S. Regs., Part II. and the Staff Manual respectively. Title pages will be prepared in manuscript.

Hour, Date, Place	Summary of Events and Information	Remarks and references to Appendices
Winchester Dec 21st 1914 8 am	Proceeded by route march to Southampton. Left Winchester to its to move at Morn Hill Camp at Southampton from lines, were formed to the Jetty from steamers. were not allowed to embark	
Southampton Dec 21 6 P.m.	Southampton to Kingstown for Havre	Precise instructions were to given to O.C. troops about rations. Also a plan of the Vessel with the names of the Officers heads to those Quarters in case of fire came to sands arranged
Havre Dec 22 2 P.m.	Disembarked at Havre. Disembarkation took a long time. Embarkation was not finished until 10 P.m. Marched to rest Camp.	
Havre Dec 23	replies from troops from Command.	
Havre Dec 24 10 am	Held the Field Ambulance to stand by at H.Q. Sheen till 11th half at 8.17. 8 P.m. Orders departure for Sebourne in loading (side) & the truck been very awkward in account of Cross beams in floor 10 ft	

1247 W 3299 200,000 (E) 8/14 J.B.C. & A. Forms/C. 2118/11.

Army Form C. 2118.

WAR DIARY
or
INTELLIGENCE SUMMARY
(Erase heading not required.)

Instructions regarding War Diaries and Intelligence Summaries are contained in F. S. Regs., Part II. and the Staff Manual respectively. Title pages will be prepared in manuscript.

Hour, Date, Place	Summary of Events and Information	Remarks and references to Appendices
Dec 24/25	*[handwritten entry, largely illegible]* Journey continued. Left Thiéceph? the halt at Abbeville. There were machines in town to thicken to fix up of the carriages to the times were only watered once by the first half. The seems only foal the halt very short. Came not able to halt the times.	
Dec 25. 2 P.M. Arques	Had half aroun[d] some billets.	
7 P.M.	Seems help to arrive	
Dec 25 h. 31" Arques	Remained at Arques. Barney in [?] charge. I lordy Thompson. Our horses are very soft & gall [?] easily. Corn & Forrage this cart to our Lerry [?] are Soft Found shortmin [?] of Colo. ["?"] Horsemans [?] aren't the main	*[signature and notes, mostly illegible]*

82ⁿᵈ Field Ambulance — 27ᵗʰ Division)

Vol I.

WAR DIARY
or
INTELLIGENCE SUMMARY

Army Form C. 2118.

Hour, Date, Place	Summary of Events and Information	Remarks and references to Appendices
Jany 1st 1915 to Jany 7 1915 Arcques	Remained at Arcques. Continues clearing habits of 82nd Brigade & No 10 & No 6 Motorbus Park at St Omer. Watch on convoy run by B Section. Received orders to proceed by Route March to Cassel.	
8 a.m. Jany 7 1915 Cassel	Proceeded by Route March to Cassel. Arrived at 3 P.M. The men found the march very difficult to march in. Their boots have begun to wear out badly. Although they have served not with a hira division of Canadian Cavalry at Winchester. These boots gave the heels badly. Hobs are already cracking, etc.	
9.15 Jany 8 1915 Cassel	Received orders to proceed by Route March to No 1 Column of 82 Brigade C. West Lake	

WAR DIARY
or
INTELLIGENCE SUMMARY

(Erase heading not required.)

Army Form C. 2118.

Hour, Date, Place	Summary of Events and Information	Remarks and references to Appendices
10 a.m. Jany 9" 1915 BOESEPPE	by route METEREN - BAILLEUL - LOCRE. Staff left owing to B & C Sections not being ready in time. We had with my traffic all the way. The Div. Am. Col. haveing in turn a halt & made the delay still worse. We had to an hour at LOCRE to allow truck transport to come through. We arrived at WESTOUTRE. I was informed that at BOESEPPE from billets have billets here at BOESEPPE at 4.0 p.m. at two farm houses. Received orders from A.D.M.S. to purchase a barbedw to fix. Orders Capt Dundas + Capt Wells with his driver to carry them out. Materiel Devries from Field Ambulance - stretchers in huts + hallcoma filled with straw	

Army Form C. 2118.

WAR DIARY
or
INTELLIGENCE SUMMARY
(Erase heading not required.)

Instructions regarding War Diaries and Intelligence Summaries are contained in F. S. Regs., Part II. and the Staff Manual respectively. Title pages will be prepared in manuscript.

Hour, Date, Place	Summary of Events and Information	Remarks and references to Appendices
BOESEPPE 9 Jany 1915	Also received orders to prepare a place for bathing & washing the men returning from the trenches. Details Capt Abeln- L. Harris & 36 men to the hotel RE are supplying hot. Cleaner up an old brewery. Wire & Barr Castor have been hot - Mr Brewery broken. 50 hot showers & a OMS Cut in two tin-mah huts. Sent Capt Abeln to Bailleul to buy towels & soap. Coldr Midy 0.5 am -5°.	
10 Jany 1915	Our Adm to Hospitals & bathing continued. Cleaning up of Egpt 8 1 farms & Alehoquin has been carried out	
11 Jany 1915	Snowed a little. 4 men went with Lt-Col Pole, to Shaw Cleaning up continued. JOLF	

WAR DIARY
or
INTELLIGENCE SUMMARY
(Erase heading not required.)

Army Form C. 2118.

Hour, Date, Place	Summary of Events and Information	Remarks and references to Appendices
Jany 12. 1915 Boesinghe	Sent two Ambulance Waggons complete to Dickebusch to assist 83rd Field Ambulance in collecting wounded	
13 – 21	Rons making. Bathing & washing continues.	
22	Others of A.O.M.S. & made a rest station. for men local school	
25	Opened rest station abendus 90 cases. "Trench feet"	
27	Change billets from farm house to villas 61 Boesinghe.	
28	1 N.C.O. & 18 men detailed to man no 7 Trench feet to (Mikerchi Battalion)	

Army Form C. 2118.

WAR DIARY
or
INTELLIGENCE SUMMARY
(Erase heading not required.)

Instructions regarding War Diaries and Intelligence Summaries are contained in F. S. Regs., Part II. and the Staff Manual respectively. Title pages will be prepared in manuscript.

Hour, Date, Place	Summary of Events and Information	Remarks and references to Appendices
Jany 30 Boeschepe	Lieut Harris & 20 men have sent to Remyshapel to open a bathing establishment	
31 "	Lieut Walsh & 15 men have sent to Westoutre to open a bathing establishment.	
Feb 1 "	Received instructions to A.D.M.S. to open another Bath in St Jacques Place. Very dirty.	
2. 3. 4 "	Cleaned out premises & formally opened new St Jacques Bath	
5	Opened No 2 Bath Station with 50 Cures.	

Army Form C. 2118.

WAR DIARY
or
INTELLIGENCE SUMMARY
(Erase heading not required.)

Instructions regarding War Diaries and Intelligence Summaries are contained in F. S. Regs., Part II. and the Staff Manual respectively. Title pages will be prepared in manuscript.

Hour, Date, Place	Summary of Events and Information	Remarks and references to Appendices
Feb 6. 27	Continued work at 82° Brigade Relay Station & two rest stations. Also continued the work of scavenging the village & remaking the roads & the sanitation & health of composite Battalion. Butcher Shop. Bath rooms. Latrines. Bath rooms. Ocean Shore Bath rooms. at various establishments. Patrol: trains 6 & 7 of February at No. 1 Rest Stat'n - 325. No 2 — 291. 4/2/ Patrol - horses through Clearing Station.	

J. L. Henryson
2nd Lt.
Can St. John Ambulance

1247 W 3290 200,000 (E) 8/14 J.B.C. & A. Forms/C. 2118/11.

121/5256
March 1915

121/5256

82nd Field Ambulance — 24th Division

Vol 44

Army Form C. 2118.

WAR DIARY
or
INTELLIGENCE SUMMARY
(Erase heading not required.)

Instructions regarding War Diaries and Intelligence Summaries are contained in F. S. Regs., Part II. and the Staff Manual respectively. Title pages will be prepared in manuscript.

Hour, Date, Place	Summary of Events and Information	Remarks and references to Appendices
BOESCHEPE 1. Mch 1915	Continued the treatment of sick at Invd Rest Stations & the 82nd Brigade Dressing Station. The cases of trench feet are falling off rapidly & sickness generally is less. Muscular Rheumatism & Hibraitis shown frequently among those sent in for treatment. The rest stations have been improved and are of great service the men returning to duty in 7 to 9 days.	
14. Mch 1915	Recd wire from A.D.M.S. to send one third of the units supply of dressings to 81st F. Ambulance.	
18. Mch 1915	Lt Col J.L. Hamilton was thrown from his horse and sustained fracture of left clavicle, sent to BAILLEUL on the 19th. Major W.H. Flint assumed command of unit.	
21 Mch "	Verbal orders recvd likely to move, evacuated all sick at rest stations	
23 " "	Recd wire from A.D.M.S. that Y.Amb is attached to 81st Bde for moves	
24 – 31	Re-opened No 2 Rest Stn Standing by with equipment packed
Patients treated during the month
82nd Bde Dressing Stn 1544
N°1 Rest Stn 262
N°2 Rest Stn 276	

[signature] Major
Commanding 80 F. Ambulance

121/5408

121/5405
April 1915

8nd Field Ambulance

S/

WAR DIARY or INTELLIGENCE SUMMARY

Army Form C. 2118.

Hour, Date, Place	Summary of Events and Information	Remarks and references to Appendices
BOESCHEPE 2. April 1915	Rec'd instructions from A.D.M.S. to proceed to YPRES to prepare rest-station	
3 April 1915	for sick. Took over École Rayant as billet at 3 P.M.	
4 "	Took the H.D. Ambce to École Rayant - YPRES with accommodation for 70 patients.	
YPRES	Left Capt. Dundas with 27 of C Co's 2 men at BOESCHEPE in charge of No 2 rest-station. Equipt & patients (49)	
5 "	Vacated École Rayant and took over Civil Hospital, where large wards allocated for sick.	
6–7.	Sent 2 officers 25 S/Ns 24 bearers to assist 83rd H.D. Amb daily	
8	Cleaning & clearing the Civil Hospital (accommodation 180 patients)	
9 "	Capt Dundas & part returned from BOESCHEPE leaving a guard of 1 o/c & 3 men.	
10 "	Rest platoon gained strength 50 o/cm.	
11 "	40 adm. 20 disch.	
12 .	Guard returned from BOESCHEPE all equipment taken on by 83rd H.D. Amb.	
	Rec'd orders to proceed to farm S.11.a. west of VLAMERTINGHE on 15th evacuate sick to 82nd & 83rd H.D. Amb at 97 c & d.	
13 .	Proud farm.	
14 "	2 Motor ambulances sent for duty to 83rd H.D. Amb	

WAR DIARY or INTELLIGENCE SUMMARY

(Erase heading not required.)

Army Form C. 2118.

Hour, Date, Place	Summary of Events and Information	Remarks and references to Appendices
VLAMERTINGHE G.11.a		
15 April 1915 8.30 P.M.	Orders rec'd for all Beard division to proceed to YPRES at once, left at 8.50 P.M. cleared up Civil Hospital which had been occupied by troops, bearers evacuated wounded from aid posts.	
17. 9 a.m.	Beard division returned from YPRES leaving one officer & one squad to collect at night in conjunction with the 81st F.A. Amb.	
18 – 23	Continued sending bearers to YPRES each night with all motor ambulances	
24/25	During action of C coy to assist No 3 Clearing Station POPERINGHE at night bearers were subjected to heavy shell fire, two bearers killed, one died of wounds, two wounded.	
	Killed. 1059 Pte Whitehurst J.N: 10959 Pte Tenny L. Died of wounds 800 Cpl Henneker G. Wounded. 760 Pte Fountacy S. Ph— Rathwell G M.T. A.S.C. B——— driver 2573 Pte Jackson C.J. 07058 Gnr Morgan A.MT & 021539 2nd Finlay R. M.T. did splendid work at the Menin bridge showing great calmness & manner in collecting, treating & evacuating a number of wounded (8) there afterwards returning to the Beard division.	
26 – 27.	Beard division continued working	
27/28 night.		

WAR DIARY
or
INTELLIGENCE SUMMARY
(Erase heading not required.)

Army Form C. 2118.

Hour, Date, Place	Summary of Events and Information	Remarks and references to Appendices
Harm G.11.a 29 April 1915. 30 9 a.m.	Rec'd instructions to send a party of men to YPRES. to bury and identify a number of dead Indian soldiers lying in the Grande Place. Sgt. Jenkins, L/Cpl Waddow and twenty men detailed with two Ford cars. on arrival the party found the Place. cleared, they were outside in heavy shell fire, the two motors were damaged as one driver of 810th HDCAM wounded and missing, three civilians were rescued from the fallen debris. Sgt. Jenkins, L/Cpl Waddow & Sawyer ASC. M.T. and men displayed great courage in carrying out their duty only leaving when the district had been thoroughly searched. L/Cpl Waddow was dressing a case in a cellar when the man struck in by falling debris, he completed the dressing, dug himself out and removed his patient.	

Signed [signature] Major
Commanding 3rd Amb.

121/5992

auto

27th Division

82nd Field Ambulance

Vol IV

May 1915. S

Army Form C. 2118.

WAR DIARY
or
INTELLIGENCE SUMMARY   82nd Field Ambulance
(Erase heading not required.)

Hour, Date, Place		Summary of Events and Information	Remarks and references to Appendices

Farm G.11.a
May 2, 1915

3.

Capt Stiles sent to dressing station. Many have been wounded in the left arm & neck presumably from a dressing station at Convent Pauline POPERINGHE under Major Wilson and 33 of Co's men accommodation for 200 cases.

1 PM — Our men were brought to the farm suffering from Gas, with news that many more were lying on the YPRES. POPERINGHE road, sent out all available ambulances (three horse) and brought in 57 cases, the oedulio carried parts of wool & Sgt Am. Cov. for inhalation which gave almost immediate relief. Symptoms: Coughing, vomiting, engorgement of R'veins of Neck & edema of Lungs. Treatment: Sgt Am. Cov. by inhalation & by the mouth. Vaseline to ease the irritation of mouth & pharynx. Oxygen for the bad cases, in about an hour all except 6 cases were completely relieved and sleeping. Next morning being quite well with no symptoms. The 6 bad cases were also wounded by shrapnel and were relieved by 5 A.M.

4.

Increased staff at POPERINGHE taken over the Annex school, and many all 2 or places to another building opposite.

During the night the heavy division in reserve passed mention, they were under heavy shell & machine gun fire, in many places they had to crawl as during the stabilities of the flares, in many cases the carry was over 3 miles all splendid.

Army Form C. 2118.

82 F Amb

WAR DIARY
or
INTELLIGENCE SUMMARY
(Erase heading not required.)

Instructions regarding War Diaries and Intelligence Summaries are contained in F. S. Regs., Part II. and the Staff Manual respectively. Title pages will be prepared in manuscript.

Hour, Date, Place	Summary of Events and Information	Remarks and references to Appendices
POPERINGHE 4/7 May. 1915		
11 P.M.	At 11 P.M. the dressing station was shelled. The first shell struck a wall of the annexe which contained 50-60 sick and lightly wounded patients a panic ensued which was cont quell by the firmness of the staff, arrangements were immediately made to evacuate all walking cases, shells of large size came at intervals of a few minutes striking the house all round so rendering stay unsafe.	
11.30	Lt. Cairns reported accumulation in a Brewery 3/4 mile away out of range.	
11.45.	Major Wilson and S/Sgt Bonges evacuated all walking cases (109) to the Brewery. Keep 247 serious cases in station. Shelling continued at intervals until 3 A.M.	
1 A.M.	All remaining cases evacuated by motor convoy. Major Blunt with Lt Cairns Sgt Hann and 3 men remained on duty at the dressing station. All ranks displayed great firmness and devotion to others during the trying time one man was killed. Pte Chippingfield R.A.M.C. 82 F. Amb. There were no casualties among the patients.	
5. May.	Opened a dressing station at the Brickfield on the POPERINGHE-ABELE road.	

Army Form C. 2118.

WAR DIARY
or
INTELLIGENCE SUMMARY
(Erase heading not required.)

82 J. A. Amb

Hour, Date, Place	Summary of Events and Information	Remarks and references to Appendices
POPERINGHE 9 May 1915. 4 P.M.	Opened a dressing station at a farm in RUE DE WESTOUTRE and established the ambulance. Lieut Major Wilson with 25 d/CB & men at the Brickfield. Bearers subjected to very heavy shell fire. Wounded :- Sgt. Dickenson Cpl Williams	
11. "	Capt Alston & 11 men recalled from C.11.a and returned to the unit.	

12. "	Draft of 2 NCOs & 11 men reported for duty at 6 P.M.
	The bearer division were again under heavy shell, rifle & machine gun fire. They were delayed 1½ hours by the ignorance of a guide as at 3 A.M. were forced to take shelter in dugouts all wounded were evacuated. The bearers returned at 10.30 A.M.
	
	Killed: 2670 Pte Duncombe J. Wounded: 2771 Pte Clout C.
	        2561 " Keelan J.S. 2678 " Sawyer C.E.
	        2518 " Poole Y.D. 2572 " Stone R.
	        1068 " Seaman W. 2721 " Hall C.
	                                                      2724 " Jenson W.
	                                                      2707 " Court J.
	                                                      2762 " Jenson W.
	
	The bearer division acted with great courage returning several times to collect the wounded, the casualties being 11 out of a total of 70.	

Army Form C. 2118.

82 F.Amb

WAR DIARY
or
INTELLIGENCE SUMMARY
(Erase heading not required.)

Hour, Date, Place	Summary of Events and Information	Remarks and references to Appendices
13.14.	Special praise is given to Pte Jacob, Pte Jenson & Thickens who were wounded, and to L/Cpl Sherringham, Pte Hood for special devn in evacuating the wounded. Pte Jacob was in charge of a squad consisting of Pte Jenson & Thickens when these latter were wounded. He carries Jenson who was wounded in both legs into safety & then returns for the patient.	
15.	Quiet night, no report.	
16 - 18.	Bearer division again under fire. no casualties.	
19th.	Quiet.	
20 - 23	9. Sgt Hill from Hdqts.	
24 - 25	Bearers divsn went to trenches at front. 9 from StaffD temp. duty to 2nd Cameron.	
26. 4 A.M.	to A & S Highlds orders rec'd to move with 82nd Brigade to 3rd Divisional Area.	
9.30 AM	orders cancelled, move rec'd.	

Army Form C. 2118.

82 Fd Amb

WAR DIARY
or
INTELLIGENCE SUMMARY
(Erase heading not required.)

Instructions regarding War Diaries and Intelligence Summaries are contained in F. S. Regs., Part II. and the Staff Manual respectively. Title pages will be prepared in manuscript.

Hour, Date, Place		Summary of Events and Information	Remarks and references to Appendices
27. May 1915. at STEENWERCK	8 AM	Warn r.c.? to be ready to move at short notice to join the 82nd Bde.	
	10.30. 4 PM	(2) order to proceed to BAILLIEUL arrived. Bailleul billets for the night.	
28 May.	6 AM.	Advance party proceed to ARMENTIERES	
	11 AM	Train party	
	2.30 PM	Arrived at Institution St Jude, ARMENTIERES and took over the building from the 18th Field Ambulance	
ARMENTIERES 29-31.		Cleaning and clearing the building	

W.H. Harris Major
82nd Field Ambulance

1247 W 2299 200,000 (E) 8/14 J.B.C. & A. Forms/C. 2118/11.

WAR DIARY
or
INTELLIGENCE SUMMARY

Army Form C. 2118.

82 Fd Amb.

Hour, Date, Place	Summary of Events and Information	Remarks and references to Appendices
82nd Field Amb. 27th Div 8 P.M. 8.6.15. ARMENTIERES.	8 P.M. Lt. Col. A.A. MARTIN, R.A.M.C.T. reported & took over the command from Major W.H. FLINT.	Admissions Wounded Offr. O.R. Sick Offr. O.R.
9.6.15.	Lt.Col. F.J. Brackenridge, D.A.D.M.S. paid visit of inspection. Advanced Dressing Stations at HOUPLINES and LE BIZET manned by O.C. with Major FLINT.	21 1
10.6.15.	Col. BROWNE, A.D.M.S. paid visit of inspection. By A.D.M.S. order officers are to wear Sam Browne belts on duty & in streets. All water for drinking to be chlorinated.	2 Lt 5
11.6.15.		
12.6.15.	All wines to be removed from men's cafés. Promotions. S. Sgt MATHER, D.G. to A/QMS vice QMS POOLE sick. 835 Sgt GRANTHAM, W.H. to 2nd A/S. Sgt. vice S.Sgt MATHER. 2523 A/Sgt ADDISON, A. to receive pay of Sgt.	17 4

Army Form C. 2118.

82 Fd Amb

WAR DIARY
or
INTELLIGENCE SUMMARY
(Erase heading not required.)

Instructions regarding War Diaries and Intelligence Summaries are contained in F. S. Regs., Part II. and the Staff Manual respectively. Title pages will be prepared in manuscript.

Hour, Date, Place	Summary of Events and Information	Remarks and references to Appendices
		S-M- wounded
		Offr OR Offr OR
		1 10 1 8
13.6.15. ARMENTIERES.	New Brigade address: 29 Rue de Dunkerque. Leave granted to Cpl Greenwood 13 June – 18th " Stevens C 16 – 21. Pte Cramp A. 18 – 23.	
14.6.15.	Order re Admissions:- All admissions to the Field Ambulance must in every case pass through the Receiving Room Draft from 2/2nd H.C. Fd Amb :- R.C. Cpl Simpson T. Pte Bampton T. Capt Fry in " SLOUGH. Joins a unit (from "SLOUGH". Capt posted to "A" Section. Capt. NAYLOR (Chaplain) went on leave.	23 1 20

Army Form C. 2118.

82 Fd Amb

WAR DIARY
or
INTELLIGENCE SUMMARY
(Erase heading not required.)

Hour, Date, Place	Summary of Events and Information	Remarks and references to Appendices
ARMENTIERES. 15.6.15.	Scabies cases no longer received here; to be sent to D. Rest Station BAC ST MAUR. Surgical went to be in charge of him to FALKINER and BORLAND. medical work in charge of Capt HOLLIS and Lieut JONES. Capt ALSTON went on leave.	Sick. wd. 2 15 3
16.6.15. 4PM	Inspection of Advance Dressing Stations at LE BIZET and HOUPLINES	1 18 3
17.6.15. 11AM	Sgt-Major BRIGHT went down "sick" to BAILLEUL. Major W.H. FLINT went down sick to BAILLEUL.	14 3
18.6.15.	Capt. C.G. BROWNE R.A.M.C. from 19th Fd. Amb. posted to this Unit for Special Duty as Adjutant for instructional purposes; posted to A. Section. S.Sgt W.A.CLENSHAW. 17844. posted to this Unit from 19th Fd Amb for instructional purposes. Pte FORD Ammed 6 A Section 18 days FP №2 for sleeping on duty.	2 21 2

Army Form C. 2118.

82nd Amb[ulance]

WAR DIARY
or
INTELLIGENCE SUMMARY
(Erase heading not required.)

Instructions regarding War Diaries and Intelligence Summaries are contained in F. S. Regs., Part II. and the Staff Manual respectively. Title pages will be prepared in manuscript.

Hour, Date, Place	Summary of Events and Information	Remarks and references to Appendices
ARMENTIERES. 19.6.'15. 11AM	Kit inspection; many deficiencies found.	Sick admissions 22 2
3PM	Inspection of Advanced Dressing Station on the Gravel, LE BIZET; deemed untenable any longer by reason of intermittent shell-fire. RUE LE BIZET chosen as Octroi House, A.D.S.	
20.6.'15.	Capt NAYLOR returned from leave. Capt H.S. HOLLIS appointed Transport Officer (MOTOR) vice Sgt. DICKINSON, N.C.O. in charge of Motor Transport. Lieut. T.A. JONES appointed Transport Officer (HORSE) with the duty of responsibility for care of respirators, smoke-helmets, & kits.	1 1st 1 1st
21.6.'15. 2PM	Inspection of Horse Transport N; deficiencies noted & individuals prepared to re-fit throughout.	15 5

Army Form C. 2118.

82 3rd Amb

WAR DIARY
or
INTELLIGENCE SUMMARY
(Erase heading not required.)

Instructions regarding War Diaries and Intelligence Summaries are contained in F.S. Regs., Part II. and the Staff Manual respectively. Title pages will be prepared in manuscript.

Hour, Date, Place	Summary of Events and Information	Remarks and references to Appendices
ARMENTIERES 22.6.'15. 6AM	Capt. ALSTON returned from leave.	Sick Held 17 1 3
11AM	Kit inspection of units, specimen kits laid out. Indents of deficiencies made out. Medical Board on Lieut **J.J.WILLIS**, 3 D.C.L.I. for fitness to serve in Regular Army. Ambulances now leave at 11:30AM and 8:15PM to remain at Adv Dressing Stn. Be light and to remain at Adv Dressing Stn.	
23.6.'15. 9AM	Lieut. FALKINER detached for duty as R.M.O. 9th R.SCOTS. vice Lieut. J.W. CAIRNS.	19 7
2:30PM	All available Officers N.C.O's visited 19th J. Amb. on the occasion of the O.C.'s weekly inspection of transport (HORSE) for instructional purposes.	

WAR DIARY or INTELLIGENCE SUMMARY

Army Form C. 2118.

82 JJ Amb

Hour, Date, Place	Summary of Events and Information	Remarks and references to Appendices
ARMENTIERES 24.6.15		Communications Sch.
10AM	C.O. opened Imprest Account; drew 4625 frs.	2 21 3
11AM	A.D.M.S. and D.A.D.M.S. paid visit of inspection.	
2PM	C.O.'s farewell.	
4PM	C.O. called on Br. de Hays; saw Col Plunkett.	
5PM	C.O. inspected 82" D.C. Baths & Fabrique Classe, six bleaching vats are used, 1 in to each 9 which pit men can get at one time; 1500 can be bathed for dinner.	
	HOUPLINES:	
25.6.15 9AM	4 changes: 1 duty Corporal "heir: 7 days C.B. 1 " lient 4 " C.B. 2 interview a Parade: Admonished	12 2
11AM	D.D.M.S (Col Skinner) visited.	
26.6.15 11:30	A.D.M.S & D.A.D.M.S visited.	
2:30	C.O., being appointed + hrs Bolund went to Bailleul for medical & surgical Stores, & to inspect No. 2 Cas. Clearing Station	11 5

Army Form C. 2118.

82 F. Amb

WAR DIARY
or
INTELLIGENCE SUMMARY
(Erase heading not required.)

Hour, Date, Place	Summary of Events and Information	Remarks and references to Appendices
ARMENTIERES		Admission
27.6.15 10.30	Church Parade in Quadrangle with Gloucester Regt.	Sick O/Rks Offr. O/Rks
8PM	C.O. & Capt. Brown selected Brewery at HOUPLINES as new advanced dressing station, in place of the one at LE BIZET to be evacuated.	20 7
28.6.15. 12 noon	A.D.M.S. & D.A.D.M.S. visited Advanced D.Sta. at LE BIZET given up. HOUPLINES occupied.	
10 A.M	C.O's inspection of horse transport:	
2.45	marked improvement since last week	
29.6.15.	C.O. called on Brigadier Gen'l Div.	
11.30	C.O's inspection of men at Dressing Sta at HOUPLINES at time of morning collection	
11.45	of sick & wounded.	

Army Form C. 2118.

WAR DIARY
or
INTELLIGENCE SUMMARY
(Erase heading not required.)

89 7th Amb

Hour, Date, Place	Summary of Events and Information	Remarks and references to Appendices
ARMENTIERES. 30.6.15. 12. Noon.	An enemy shell struck a stable used by us on the side of the road opposite H.Q'rs, wrecking the stove-room where one of the men was cleaning harness. He had a narrow escape but beyond the shock seemed little the worse. Five minutes later another shell fell through the roof of the large pavilion used as Medical Ward where there were eleven men in bed; the shell burst between the roof and the ceiling inflicting slight wounds on nine patients and more or less shock on them all. They were all removed at once, first to the Surgical Ward & then to the	

Army Form C. 2118.

89 7a Amb

WAR DIARY
or
INTELLIGENCE SUMMARY
(Erase heading not required.)

Hour, Date, Place	Summary of Events and Information	Remarks and references to Appendices
ARMENTIERES 12 Noon 30.6.15.	Spacious cellar beneath entrance hall. All the patients were in the cellar which was lit-by candles & lamps: dinner was served there & all patients remained there for 2 hours, when the shelling ceased. The hole in the roof of ward was repaired as far as possible, in a temporary fashion. The aperture of ingress of shell in the Zinc roofing material shews it have been 3½ inches or 90 m.m. in diameter: it was probably high-explosive-shrapnel. All lying cases evacuated to BAILLEUL C.C.S. 3 P.M.	A H Macintosh Col O.C. 82 F. Amb

1247 W 3299 200,000 (E) S/14 J.B. & A. Forms/C. 2118/11.

27th Division

121/6443

82nd Field Ambulance

Vol V

From 1st to 31st July 1915

121/6443

July '15

WAR DIARY or INTELLIGENCE SUMMARY

Army Form C. 2118.

(Erase heading not required.)

Instructions regarding War Diaries and Intelligence Summaries are contained in F. S. Regs., Part II. and the Staff Manual respectively. Title pages will be prepared in manuscript.

Hour, Date, Place	Summary of Events and Information	Remarks and references to Appendices
ARMENTIERES.		Admissions / Sick OR / Wounded Officer / OR
1 July 15. 11 AM.	No repetition of bombardment. D.A.D.M.S. Watson inspected damaged sand & stable.	2 / 9 / 1 / 2
2.7.15. 11 AM.	A.D.M.S. visited; inspected damaged wash & stable.	1 / 11 / – / 1
3.7.15. 11.30 AM.	Formal inspection by Col. Rattray, O.C. 19 Amb. on occasion of General Kerr's inspection.	1 / 3 / – / 3
4.7.15. 3 PM.	D.D.M.S. (Col. Stevens) visited & inspected premises.	– / 6 / – / 4
5.7.15. 2 PM.	Inspection of horse-transport by A.D.M.S., D.A.D.M.S. (Col Rattray, O.C. 19 & 7 Amb. also present). Much improvement noted. Anti rat infection.	– / 6 / – / 1
5 PM.	Draft of 5 men arrived from 2/2nd H.C./9 Amb. viz 28/2 Pte Rye A.; 306 Pte Williams T.; 2958 Pte Josey A. (adot); Pte Dennis J. (son); 298 Pte Botts C.g. (15 Sect).	

Forms/C. 2118/11 1/97.

WAR DIARY
or
INTELLIGENCE SUMMARY

(Erase heading not required.)

Army Form C. 2118.

Hour, Date, Place	Summary of Events and Information	Remarks and references to Appendices
ARMENTIERES 6.7.15 11.30 AM	General Inspection of Unit by A.D.M.S. (D.A.D.M.S. wanted the O.C.)	Sick Off OR 9
8.30 AM	5 men of PPCLI brought in suffering from shell wounds having been struck while standing in the doorway of their billet in the town near the Ambulance H.Qrs. One man had a large hole blown out of side of skull + shortly died; others slightly 4.7.15	2 — 11
8.7.15 3PM	Capt Dundas left to take up Sanitary duties at Dieppe. Capt. Alston instructed to carry on duties as respirator officer.	8 — 1
9.7.15	Major Hunt's sick leave extended till 23rd July.	14 — 8
10.7.15 3PM	Lieut Cairns went on leave. A.D.M.S. issued verbal instruction re care of horses.	3 — 11

O.M. Conroll in Earle nativale, Rev. Rev. Naylor. C.F.

Army Form C. 2118.

WAR DIARY
— on —
INTELLIGENCE SUMMARY
(Erase heading not required.)

Instructions regarding War Diaries and Intelligence Summaries are contained in F. S. Regs., Part II. and the Staff Manual respectively. Title pages will be prepared in manuscript.

Hour, Date, Place	Summary of Events and Information	Remarks and references to Appendices
ARMENTIERES. 11.7.15. 9 PM	C.O., sent to A.D.M.S. proposals regarding division of Unit: A + B Sections with all motors to stay in Town. C. Section with its equipment to go to a camp under canvas, N.W. of River LYS.	admissions Sick O.R. Wounded O.R. 1 8 3
11 AM	Reconnaissance of terrain in district chosen for camp, by C.O's of the Ambulances of the Division, with Capt. Williamson, acting D.A.D.M.S.	
12.7.15. 12 noon	Enemy shells falling in town quite near H.qrs. Patients sent down into large cellar under entrance hall for 1½ hours.	7 4
13.7.15. 11 AM	A.D.M.S. & Acting D.A.D.M.S. visited. Question of status of H. Transport Section now discussed; whether they may be R.A.M.C. or A.S.C. They are to be considered A.S.C.	1 8 4

Forms/C. 2118/11.

1247 W 3299 200,000 (E) 8/14 J.B.C. & A.

Army Form C. 2118.

WAR DIARY
INTELLIGENCE SUMMARY

(Erase heading not required.)

Instructions regarding War Diaries and Intelligence Summaries are contained in F. S. Regs., Part II. and the Staff Manual respectively. Title pages will be prepared in manuscript.

Hour, Date, Place	Summary of Events and Information	Remarks and references to Appendices
ARMENTIERES 13.7.15. 9 P.M.	Visited A.D.M.S. on Hqrs. and received verbal orders to move the Unit from ARMENTIERES at 10 A.M. on 14th inst — leaving patients with 83rd F. Amb.	Sick Offrs O.R. Offrs. O.R. 7 3
14.7.15 8 A.M.	Unit moved off complete, + marched via PONT DE NIEPPE with two halts to FERME ROSIÈRE (sheet 36c. B.26.b.6.8) where it went to bivouac. Move completed at 12 noon.	
2 P.M.	Afternoon spent — arranging bivouacs + erecting marquee + hospital tents for 20 patients.	
3.30 P.M.	A.D.M.S. & acting D.A.D.M.S. visited.	
15.7.15.	Very heavy rain (estimated one inch) during night. Fatigue work in elaborating camps + bivouacs. Lieut F. SCROGGIE arrived from 2/2nd Home Counties Fd. Amb. (second line Unit in England).	0 0 (Patients temporarily handed over to 83rd F. Amb.)

Army Form C. 2118.

WAR DIARY
or
INTELLIGENCE SUMMARY

(Erase heading not required.)

Instructions regarding War Diaries and Intelligence Summaries are contained in F. S. Regs., Part II. and the Staff Manual respectively. Title pages will be prepared in manuscript.

Hour, Date, Place	Summary of Events and Information	Remarks and references to Appendices
FERME ROSIERE (WATERLANDS) Sheet 36: B.26.6.6.8 16.7.15.		admissions
7.A.M.	All R.M.O's of Bde visited by C.O. Infantry units now bivouacs in fields in neighbourhood – resting.	Sick 4 ORs
11 A.M.	Patients taken over from 83rd F. Amb. Lieut Jones returned from R.M.O. duty.	wounded officers OR 1
		3
17.7.15. 10 A.M.	Lieut Scroggie detailed to do R.M.O. duty to 8th Heavy Battery R.G.A.	
	11 A.M. C.O. called at Bde Hqrs at ERQUINGHAM for general instructions.	2
4 P.M.	A.D.M.S. visited. Adjoining farm taken over by Unit in addition to FERME ROSIERE.	
18.7.15. 3 P.M.	D.A.D.M.S. visited + ordered that one section complete move to mothers should go to FORT ROMPU (Sheet 36. H.7.d) on the ERQUINGHAM – SAILLY road at noon 19th inst. C.O. called on O/C MAC[?] at MERVILLE to arrange routine of calls as from 19th inst vice 9th M.A. Convoy from BAILLEUL. 9th M.A.Conv[?] also moves to LA GORGUE near ESTAIRES.	9

Forms/C.2118/11

1247 W 3299 200,000 (E) 8/14 J.B.C. & A.

WAR DIARY
INTELLIGENCE SUMMARY
(Erase heading not required.)

Army Form C. 2118.

Instructions regarding War Diaries and Intelligence Summaries are contained in F. S. Regs., Part II. and the Staff Manual respectively. Title pages will be prepared in manuscript.

Hour, Date, Place	Summary of Events and Information	Remarks and references to Appendices
FERME ROSIÈRE 19.7.75. 10.30 A.M.	B. Section (Major G.T. MILLAN, Capt. HOLLIS, + Lts. + JONES) moved up to occupy FORT ROMPU. Lieut PIPER & 83rd F. Amb. also went with the section as he knew the positions of all the Regimental Aid Posts from previously working in the area.	Sick Admissions o/rs OR o/rs OR o/rs OR 5
20.7.15.	Brewery at Mon Rompu fitted up for patients, accommodation good. A.D.M.S. marked both stations. Advanced dressing station located at GRIS POT (sheet 36. H.18). The Regt Aid Posts being at BOIS GRENIER + LA VESÉE (I.19). O.C. visited all R.A.P's at BOIS GRENIER this have fell + there is Rain; O/shed. Right knee deeply grazed over + considerable area. Out left ankle slightly sprained, but able to note back & spokes.	33 1

Forms/C. 2118/11.

WAR DIARY
or
INTELLIGENCE SUMMARY
(Erase heading not required.)

Army Form C. 2118.

Hour, Date, Place	Summary of Events and Information	Remarks and references to Appendices
FERME ROSIÈRE 22.7.15. 11AM	Capt. P. WOOD. R.A.M.C. arrived for duty from 26th Base Hosp-l at ETAPLES.	Admissions Sick Micer OR OR OR
		22/7/15 14
3.30	Major General MILNE; C.B., D.S.O., inspected Unit at horse stations. Shoeing & horses criticised: too much paring of hoofs at heels and too little at toe of hoofs, causing too much pressure on the frog.	22.7.15 12 1 2
24.7.15. 10AM	Veterinary Officer (Lieut. Turnbull) visited all sections: to inspect horses' hoofs & shoes; separate shoeing books to be kept for each section	23.7.15 10 1 3
		10
4PM	Lt. Col. Riddell A.S.C. visited.	
5PM	D.A.D. u. S. visited.	
25.7.15 2PM	Lieut. Boland went on leave	13 1

WAR DIARY or INTELLIGENCE SUMMARY

(Erase heading not required.)

Army Form C. 2118.

Instructions regarding War Diaries and Intelligence Summaries are contained in F.S. Regs., Part II. and the Staff Manual respectively. Title pages will be prepared in manuscript.

Hour, Date, Place	Summary of Events and Information	Remarks and references to Appendices
FERME ROSIÈRE. 26.7.15. 10AM	General working parties to clean ditches in vicinity of billets. Fire Shuffle detailed t R.I.Que to hutments Bailleuls (on leave). Numerous fragments of shells fell in the camp from anti-aircraft guns firing at Taube overhead; no casualties.	Sick Officers Wounded O.R. O.R. ORs Africa — 16 — 8/fr 4
27.7.15. 10A.M.	Ditch cleaning work continued.	10 — — 7
28.7.15. 2.30 3.30	Inspection of Horse Transport: general condition excellent. A.D.M.S. visited.	16 — — 1
29.7.15. 2PM	C.O's inspection; general state of personnel good. New two-trail latrines arranged for the men: new Solid matter tubs burned in a new incinerator.	10 — — 1
30.7.15. 11AM 2PM	100 ft drawn from the Cadres (English). Kit Inspection. Pay parade and smoke-helmet inspection & spraying.	6 — — 2
31.7.15.	A.D.M.S. visited: C.O. and Q.M. went over to PIGEON FARM near STEENWERCK to examine site for new camp if needed.	4 — — 4
		Total for July 295 5 — 74

A.A. Hulst. Lt-Col. RAMC O.C. 82 F.Amb.

Forms/C. 2118/11.

121/6598

27th Division

82nd Field Ambulance
Vol VI
From 1 - 31. 8. 15

August 1915

Army Form C. 2118.

WAR DIARY
or
INTELLIGENCE SUMMARY
(Erase heading not required.)

Hour, Date, Place	Summary of Events and Information	Remarks and references to Appendices
FERME ROSTIÈRE 1.8.'15.	Chaplain attached to this Unit — the Rev'd A.T.A.Naylor — held thirteen services at various points in the Brigade Area, ministering to twenty four Units, Batteries, etc; the work of this officer meets the highest possible praise, and is often carried out under most hazardous conditions.	
2.8.'15 8AM	A' Section of 61st F. Amb. joined B. Section of this Unit at FORT ROMPU (BRASSERIE) for a week's instruction; officers:— Major Harvey,	
3 (?)PM 2 PM	2nd Lieut. CAIRNS returned from R.M.O duty. At the FARM the afternoon was observed as a Bank Holiday and a cricket match between A' section v an outgoing field A. warn C. Section: A' section won by eight runs.	
6 PM	Open-air Concert.	

1247 W 3299 200,000 (E) 8/14 J.B.C. & A. Forms/C. 2118/11.

WAR DIARY
or
INTELLIGENCE SUMMARY

(Erase heading not required.)

Army Form C. 2118.

Hour, Date, Place	Summary of Events and Information	Remarks and references to Appendices
FERME ROSIÈRE 3.8.15. 6AM	Lieut Borland returned from leave.	
5-8-'15	Major F.W. FLINT returned from England and was posted for temp duty to 83rd & 7th Amb. from Field Ambce	
6-8-'15 3PM	A.D.M.S. visited accompanied by Inspector (OC, 61 & 7 Amb.) to discuss farming of A Section 61 Fd Ambce.	
7.		
8.		
9. 9AM	A Section 61st Fd Amb left Fort Rompu to report Unit	
10-8 8AM	B Section 61 & 9 Amb arrived at Fort Rompu	
11 12No	Lieut SCROGGIE returned from R.M.O. duty.	
2PM	D.R. Col. A.A. MARTIN left for ENGLAND. I handed over the command to Lt Col A.A.Wrath Lt Col	

MAJOR R GT WILLAN

WAR DIARY
or
INTELLIGENCE SUMMARY

Army Form C. 2118.

Hour, Date, Place	Summary of Events and Information	Remarks and references to Appendices
FERME ROSIÈRE 12/8/15 10 AM	C.O. visited Field Cashier at ERQUINGHEM and handed over balance of Imprest account. Fresh Imprest account drawn. Captain H.S. HOLLIS is appointed to command B Section.	
13/8/15 10.30 AM	ADMS & DADMS call and take C.O. and Lieut Q.M. HARRIS to visit large farm at L'ESTRADE, near STEENWERCK. The farm consists of the usual square of buildings with manure dump in the middle, most of the buildings are recent & not quite completed as regards floors, doors, windows; a large barn on the South side is of older date; and outside is a Quaker barn with corrugated iron roof and iron supports. It is decided to take it over and complete it so that it act to take a complete field ambulance and patients. Cn. Yd. G.T.N	

1247 W 3299 200,000 (E) 8/14 J.B.C. & A. Forms/C. 2118/11.

WAR DIARY
or
INTELLIGENCE SUMMARY
(Erase heading not required.)

Army Form C. 2118.

Hour, Date, Place	Summary of Events and Information	Remarks and references to Appendices
FERME ROSIÈRE		
13/8/15 – (cont'd) 5.30 p.m.	Party of 2 N.C.O.'s (Sergt Ingleton i/c) and 25 men sent to start work at L'ESTRADE and billet there. The N.C.O. and six men withdrawn from PIGEON FARM.	G.T.R.
14/8/15	Lieut. & Qr.Mr. G.W. HARRIS drew up plans showing proposed arrangements and alterations he made at L'ESTRADE, this is forwarded to A.D.M.S. this afternoon.	G.T.R.
15/8/15	Work proceeded. A further working party of 30 men sent to clear ditches &c at L'ESTRADE.	
16/8/15 – 7.0 A.M.	C.O. with Capt. WOOD rode to GRISPOT trenches. Advanced Dressing Station there before handing over to 87 Field Ambulance.	
9.0 p.m.	82nd Infantry Brigade leave trenches for 2 weeks rest in billets.	G.T.R.

WAR DIARY or INTELLIGENCE SUMMARY

(Erase heading not required.)

Army Form C. 2118.

Hour, Date, Place	Summary of Events and Information	Remarks and references to Appendices
FERME ROSIÈRE. 17-8-15 9.0AM	Captⁿ QUINN with B Section GMR Flashiana on completion of a weeks instruction work and leave return from FORT ROMPU to their Unit.	
3.0 pm	Captain H.S. HOLLIS with Lieuts CAIRNS & SCROGGIE and B Section 82nd F.A. Ambulance return here, handing over the Dressing Station at FORT ROMPU and Advanced Dressing Station at GRIS-POT to Major PEYTON and B Section of 81st Field Ambulance.	
4.0 pm	Captain MACKENZIE R.A.M.C. (TC) arrives here for duty from INDIAN CORPS. and is posted temporarily to B Section.	E.S.R.
18-8-15	A medical officer with an orderly and a motor ambulance detailed daily as required to attend 2nd Divisional Grenadier School at LA BOUDRELLE. He is only required when detonators or live bombs are practised with.	
2.0 pm	Captain MACKENZIE leaves for United Kingdom for 14 days leave.	
	Captain DELGARDO. M.O. i/c 1st Leinster Reg^t leaves for United Kingdom on 7 days leave.	
	Captain H.S. HOLLIS takes over temporary Medical Charge of 1st Leinster Reg^t. E.S.R.	

Army Form C. 2118.

WAR DIARY
or
INTELLIGENCE SUMMARY
(Erase heading not required.)

Instructions regarding War Diaries and Intelligence Summaries are contained in F.S. Regs., Part II. and the Staff Manual respectively. Title pages will be prepared in manuscript.

Hour, Date, Place	Summary of Events and Information	Remarks and references to Appendices
FERME ROSIÈRE		
19-8-15. 2.0pm	Captain W.E. ALSTON leaves the unit for ENGLAND being posted for duty with the 2/2 Home Counties Field Ambulance. Lieut SCROGGIE takes over duties of Brigade Sanitary Officer. LIEUT. J. CAIRNS is appointed to take command of C. Section.	
20-8-15. 2.0pm	C.O. inspects Sanitary Arrangements at the 82nd Tn⁵ Bgde Transport Lines; finds new latrines, urinals, and ablution places under process of construction, and under supervision of the Divisional Sanitary Officer LIEUT. WHITE (TF) his new. The method of incineration of all local matters has been adopted also in use by all units in the Division.	
3.30pm	Col. BRUCE SKINNER A.M.S. D.D.M.S 3rd Corps visits and inspects Camp; discusses means for preventing waste of rations; informed him regret that was no longer useful FORT ROMPU. S.K.W.	

1247 W 3299 200,000 (E) 8/14 J.B.C.&A. Forms/C. 2118/11.

Army Form C. 2118.

WAR DIARY
or
INTELLIGENCE SUMMARY
(Erase heading not required.)

Instructions regarding War Diaries and Intelligence Summaries are contained in F. S. Regs., Part II. and the Staff Manual respectively. Title pages will be prepared in manuscript.

Hour, Date, Place	Summary of Events and Information	Remarks and references to Appendices
FERME ROSIÈRE 21-8-15. 10.0AM	C.O. attended conference at ADMS' office with O.C. 51st & 83rd Field Ambulances and the A.P.M. Major BRIERLEY on General Diseases and the methods to be used in notification and dealing with the sources of infection in the Divisional area.	
2.0 p.m.	Lieut & QM G.W. HARRIS proceeds to United Kingdom for 7 days leave; during his absence his duties will be performed by Quartermaster Sergeant MATHER.	G.T.W.
22-8-15. 10 AM	All officers and men of the unit under the C.O. attended 82nd Brigade Church Parade on the recreation ground near ERQUINGHEM BRIDGE.	
5.30 p.m.	Major F.G. BUSHNELL RAMC (TF) from 2nd Eastern General Hospital Brighton arrived and is attached temporarily for work and for duty.	G.T.W.

WAR DIARY or INTELLIGENCE SUMMARY

Army Form C. 2118.

Hour, Date, Place	Summary of Events and Information	Remarks and references to Appendices
FERME ROSIÈRE.		
23-8-15. 11.0AM	ADVS 27th Division inspects horses of the unit, recommends better methods of protecting horses. Supply H.Q. cannot be tied up to ordinary lines; he found the strong marred where few cases shoes were a bit short.	
4.30pm	O.O. inspects work at L'ESTRADE. Good progress made, in new brickwork for floors & water washing. Manure dumps dug out and arrangements made to thoroughly drain it. Cover it of with freer earth.	
24-8-15.	Harvesting parties of from 2—8 men lent daily to neighbouring farmers; the a.a. chosen appreciate the change of their help is very gratefully acknowledged.	G.F.W.

Army Form C. 2118.

WAR DIARY
or
INTELLIGENCE SUMMARY
(Erase heading not required.)

Instructions regarding War Diaries and Intelligence Summaries are contained in F. S. Regs., Part II. and the Staff Manual respectively. Title pages will be prepared in manuscript.

Hour, Date, Place	Summary of Events and Information	Remarks and references to Appendices
FERME ROSIÈRE 25-8-15 - 2.30pm	Transport Competition between 4 Field Ambulances - the 36th Bgde P2d & 83rd were held at ERQUINGHEM. and of 8 Events 6 First Prizes & 2 Seconds were won by 82nd Field Ambulance.	G.Th.
26-8-15 3.30pm	Lieuts COCK and WALLACE R.A.M.C. (T.C.) arrive from the base and are posted temporarily to B & C Section respectively.	G.Th.
27-8-15 10.0 AM	C.O. with Lieut. J. CAIRNS visits Dressing Station at ERQUINGHEM and receives much information from Captain STURROCK of 83rd Field Ambulance about the arrangements there. The C.O. considers the transport in to be far away from the Hospital.	G.Th.
28-8-15 10.50 AM	C.O. visits L'ESTRADE, great improvement noted; a large letter held by Sergt. INGLETON & Carpenter to find a cow to billet on First Floor afraid from Horse Lines, the lucky fortune not having arrived, the form is vainly read, & receipt ston-	G.Th.

Army Form C. 2118.

WAR DIARY
or
INTELLIGENCE SUMMARY

(Erase heading not required.)

Instructions regarding War Diaries and Intelligence Summaries are contained in F. S. Regs., Part II. and the Staff Manual respectively. Title pages will be prepared in manuscript.

Hour, Date, Place	Summary of Events and Information	Remarks and references to Appendices
FERME ROSIÈRE 29-8-15. 10.0 AM	82nd Brigade Church Parade at ERQUINGHEM, all Candidates N.C.O.s & men of the unit attached under command of Captain H.S. HOLLIS.	S.T.W.
2.30 pm	CO visited 82nd I. Brigade Head Quarters & found out disposition of troops in taking over & put had portion of the line on the 30th inst. Medical arrangements made accordingly and orders re collection and evacuation of casualties sent to the R.M.O.s of the Brigade.	appendix I copy of medical arrangements for 82nd Infantry Brigade by Major G. Trestrail S.M.O. S.T.W.
10.30 AM	Major F.G. BUSHNELL. RAMC(TF) under orders from ADMS leaves to take over Medical Charge of Troops at VIEUX BERQUIN reports on arrival to O/C Ammunition Supply Park 3rd Corps	S.T.W.

Army Form C. 2118.

WAR DIARY
or
INTELLIGENCE SUMMARY
(Erase heading not required.)

Instructions regarding War Diaries and Intelligence Summaries are contained in F. S. Regs., Part II. and the Staff Manual respectively. Title pages will be prepared in manuscript.

Hour, Date, Place	Summary of Events and Information	Remarks and references to Appendices
FERME ROSIÈRE 30-8-15 10.0 AM	LIEUT. COCK is appointed to take over medical charge of the 1st Royal Irish Regt. in place of LIEUT. J.T. DICKSON proceeding to the United Kingdom on 7 days leave.	
2.0 pm	LIEUT. WALLACE proceeds to take over Advanced Dressing Station at corner of road leading into RUE MARLE (Sheet 36. H.6.d.8.6) from Captain PYPER 83rd Field Ambulance.	
	CAPTAIN. H.G. MONTEITH. RAMC M.O/c 2nd D.C.L.I's is appointed to take over charge of sick and sanitation at 82nd Brigade Head Quarters in addition to his regimental duties.	
		C.W.J.S.
31-8-15 8.0 AM	On A.D.O. 2 11 men of C.Section with equipment, two wheeled stretcher carrier take leave & join LIEUT. WALLACE at Advanced Dressing Station relieving men from 83rd Field Amb in Motor Ambulance being returned thence for duty.	
		G.T.W.
		C.W.J.S.

Army Form C. 2118.

WAR DIARY
or
INTELLIGENCE SUMMARY
(Erase heading not required.)

Hour, Date, Place	Summary of Events and Information	Remarks and references to Appendices
FERME ROSIERE. 21-8-15 Cont.		
9.0 AM	C Section under LIEUT J CAIRNS with LIEUT SCROGGIE, proceed to ERQUINCHEM to take over Dressing Station there from C Section of F S U Field Ambulance. Two large motor ambulances and one FORD are the stationed there. Space being found for them to stand just outside the north gate of Hospital yard. Position of Dressing Station is Sheet 36 H.4.d.4.9. Space for horse lines has been found in large field just across the main road and additional stabling at the Bakers just West of the Hospital.	
2.30 pm	Lieut. Col. LIDDELL. ASC o/c Divisional Train with staff unloaded the Horse Transport of their ambulance which was on parade at the time.	
5.0 pm	Captain H.S. HOLLIS instructed to join LIEUT WALLACE at advanced Dressing Station, remaining there for 3 days.	

G.T. McClan Major.
RAMC (T)

Appendix I.
Copy of Medical Arrangements for 82nd I. Bgde
by Major G T Willan
S.M.O

To M.O. i/c ....

Medical Arrangements for 82° Infantry Brigade.

Until further notice 82° Field Ambulance Dressing Station will be at **ERQUINGHAM LYS** at H: h: d: (Sheet 36)

Advanced Dressing Station near corner of road leading into **RUE MARLE** at H.6. d. 8:6: (Sheet 36)

Billets.

Each morning a car will collect from billets at 10.30. a.m. all cases of sickness unable to walk to Advanced Dressing Station.

Walking cases should be at advanced Dressing Station by 10.30. a.m.

Regimental Aid Posts.

R.M.O's. will telephone to Advanced Dressing Station by 5 p.m. nightly giving number and description (sitting or lying) of cases awaiting evacuation.

Cases of extreme urgency will be collected at any time upon notification being received.

R.M.O.'s should conform strictly to these times to facilitate collection.

G. T. Willan.

29/8/15.

Major. R.A.M.C.
Commanding 82° Field Ambce.

121/7050

27/h/Swann

82nd Field Ambulance

Vol XII

Sept. 15

Sep 15.

WAR DIARY
or
INTELLIGENCE SUMMARY
(Erase heading not required.)

Army Form C. 2118.

Hour, Date, Place	Summary of Events and Information	Remarks and references to Appendices
FERME ROSIÈRE. 1-9-15. 2.0 pm	C.O. inspects A & B Sections. Weather changed, much cooler and some rain. One blanket per man indented for in accordance with D.R.O. 524 of 30/8/15. G.T.W.	
2-9-15. 5.30 AM	Capt'n MACKENZIE returns from leave.	
2.0 pm	C.O. with Lieut CAIRNS rode to the Advanced Dressing Station which is formed in a refugee factory near corner of road leading into the RUE MARLE (Sheet 36. H.6.W.6.6.) from there accompanied by Captain H.S. HOLLIS (who is in charge a visit is made to the Regimental aid Posts of the 1st Cambridge Reg't and the 2nd D.C.L.I. the route taken being to the LILLE Road and down that to wards CHAPELLE ARMENTIÈRES as far as the Railway crossing where the Motor Ambulances are left — cont'd	

WAR DIARY
or
INTELLIGENCE SUMMARY
(Erase heading not required.)

Army Form C. 2118.

Hour, Date, Place	Summary of Events and Information	Remarks and references to Appendices
2-9-15 cnt^d	The rest of the journey being made on foot along a path by the side of the railway as far as the road crossing were taking the road to the left. The avenues (communicating trenches) begin; these are wide tortuous and well drained trenches and the Aid Posts are in them about 50 yards in the rear of the Support Trenches where the Battalion Head Quarters are situated; the avenues being continued forward into the fire trenches. The Aid Posts are dug outs well roofed and protected from shrapnel & shrapnel shell fire. Heavy rain coming in parents a road to the Aid Post of the Royal Irish Reg^t. 2 Casualties from shell fire in the RUE de LILLE were admitted to Dressing Station. G.T.W.	

WAR DIARY
or
INTELLIGENCE SUMMARY

(Erase heading not required.)

Army Form C. 2118.

Hour, Date, Place	Summary of Events and Information	Remarks and references to Appendices
FERME ROSIÈRE 3-9-15- 2.30pm	C.O. with MAJOR MACKENZIE, O.C. 53rd Field Ambulance told his Quartermaster visits the farm at L'ESTRADE to discuss the accommodation there for two head quarters and 3 Sections of a Field Ambulance, and arrangement now for transport of more than one unit	
5.20pm	C.O. & Captain H.S. HOLLIS & LIEUT. J.W. CAIRNS visit A.D.M.S' office for conference with D.A.D.M.S. and officer of the other Field Ambulances, subject being the 24th Divisional Defence Scheme. Weather – been wet & cold.	
8.20pm	Letter from A.D.M.S. Enquire into her farm at L'ESTRADE by noon on the 5th inst.	G.P.W.
4-9-15- 10.0AM	C.O. & Sergt Major CLENSHAW visit L'ESTRADE to make arrangements for its completion by A. & B. Sections	G.P.W.
6.0.pm	Captn A.A. SEATON 1st Camb. died of wounds at Dressing Station	G.P.W.

Army Form C. 2118.

WAR DIARY
or
INTELLIGENCE SUMMARY
(Erase heading not required.)

Instructions regarding War Diaries and Intelligence Summaries are contained in F. S. Regs., Part II. and the Staff Manual respectively. Title pages will be prepared in manuscript.

Hour, Date, Place	Summary of Events and Information	Remarks and references to Appendices
5-9-15		
6.30 AM	All tents struck & wagons packed.	
10.0 AM	A & B Sections, less an officer & N.C.O. & 6 men who are left to clear up the ground, leave FERME ROSIÈRE and march to new quarters at L'ESTRADE (sheet 36 A.30.6.Y.Y.) arriving without a halt at 10.40 A.M. The transport under Capt. R. Wood arriving at 10.55 A.M as they had to make a detour towards CROIX-du-BAC owing to the road to MENEGATE being closed to traffic proceeding from south to north.	
2.45 pm	C.O. visits Dressing Station at ERQUINGHEM holds conference on the Divisional Defence Scheme with 3 officers of the unit and the R.M.O's of R. Ir. Fusiliers and 1st Leinster Regt. Lieut. VENABLES & Capt. DELGARDO.	
	cont'd.	

WAR DIARY
or
INTELLIGENCE SUMMARY
(Erase heading not required.)

Army Form C. 2118.

Hour, Date, Place	Summary of Events and Information	Remarks and references to Appendices
L'ESTRADE.		
5-9-15 Cont'd		
5.0 pm	A French Stretcher despatched by Capt'n. MAGNER 9 m O/C 1st Cambridge Reg't. is forwarded to A.D.M.S.	G.F.W.
6-9-15.	Weather changed to finer, clearer, & warmer sun shine	
9.20 AM	Col. EVERETT, C.B. visits and inspects Farm.	
4.0 pm	Col. BRUCE SKINNER, D.D.M.S. visits and inspects " "	
4.45 pm	Major COLLEN " " Farm	
5.30 pm	D.A.D.M.S. " " "	
	During the morning while a Company of the Munsters was marching down the Road ARMENTIÈRES — WEZ MACQUART, in (Sheet 36) I 8 a Shrapnel shell killed one and wounded eleven, the road being subsequently closed to all traffic in daylight.	G.F.W.

Army Form C. 2118.

WAR DIARY
INTELLIGENCE SUMMARY
(Erase heading not required.)

Instructions regarding War Diaries and Intelligence Summaries are contained in F.S. Regs., Part II. and the Staff Manual respectively. Title pages will be prepared in manuscript.

Hour, Date, Place	Summary of Events and Information	Remarks and references to Appendices
L'ESTRADE		
7-9-15: 5.30 AM	Lieut. J.T. DIXON returns from Leave and resumes medical charge of 1st Royal Irish Regt. Lieut. COCK returns for duty with the Field Ambulance.	
2.0 pm	An N.C.O. and twenty men are detailed for work on the farm of VEUVE CREPIN at L'HALLOBEAU.	G.T.W.
8-9-15: 8.30 AM	Six marquee tents and 5 bell tents with fittings party sent to Divisional Grenadier School.	
10.0 AM	C.O. visits DADMS Lieut. Col. F.J. BRACKENRIDGE who has received an appointment and is leaving to join the 12th Corps. His departure is much regretted by all ranks.	
4.30 pm	Two Green, 4 N.C.O's and 15 men of 70th Field Ambulance 23rd Division arrive for instruction at Dressing Station at ERQUINGHEM.	G.T.W.

WAR DIARY
or
INTELLIGENCE SUMMARY

(Erase heading not required.)

Army Form C. 2118.

Instructions regarding War Diaries and Intelligence Summaries are contained in F.S. Regs., Part II. and the Staff Manual respectively. Title pages will be prepared in manuscript.

Hour, Date, Place	Summary of Events and Information	Remarks and references to Appendices
L'ESTRADE.		
9-9-15		
10 AM	C.O. visit ERQUINGHEM Rumbeek Dressing Station. Finds wards and billets clean & very well kept.	
	Captn H.G. MONTEITH, D.S.O. R.A.M.C. NFO i/c 2nd D.C.L.I. is to be heartily congratulated on his well deserved honour; on proceeding on leave the united brethren his work is taken over temporarily by Captn MACKENZIE. R.A.M.C.	
10-9-15		
10.30 AM	To my general regret on Chaplain Captn the Rev. C.E. NAYLOR C of E. has to be evacuated sick, his illness being caused by long hours in the Saddle in pursuit of his duties	g.v.w.
11-9-15		
12.30 PM	Major J. WARD. R.A.M.C.T. Acting A.D.M.S and Cpln RUDKIN. R.A.M.C on new D.A.D.M.S visit L'ESTRADE	g.v.w.
		Cmtd

WAR DIARY
or
INTELLIGENCE SUMMARY
(Erase heading not required.)

Army Form C. 2118.

Hour, Date, Place	Summary of Events and Information	Remarks and references to Appendices
L'ESTRADE		
11-9-15 Cont'd	A new batch of 40 to Field Ambulance, 2 officers & 15 men arrive at Dressing Station for a few days instruction, the first party returning (this . . .) &c.	
12-9-15. 3.0.p.m.	C.O. inspects Transport lines of 82nd Inf. Brigade. &c.	
4.0 p.m.	Divine Service (c/E) held in large barn. &c.	
13-9-15. 4.0 AM	A German biplane after being shelled by our anti aircraft guns is attacked by an allied airman (both using machine guns) & forced to descend. the machine an Albatros No. 853 (MILITAAR. ZEIG ZUNG C.45/15) after a tremendous vol plane was safely brought to earth in ploughed land.	

Army Form C. 2118.

WAR DIARY
or
INTELLIGENCE SUMMARY
(Erase heading not required.)

Hour, Date, Place	Summary of Events and Information	Remarks and references to Appendices
L'ESTRADE 13-9-15	English - fields 600 yds north of here close to outskirts of STEENWEREK. On landing there was a few outbreak of machine gun & rifle fire and on seeing that it was found that the firemen had turned their machine gun on the company of K.R.R. Coln on the STEENWEREK - CROIX DU BAC Rd who replied killing both the Germans and also unfortunately one of their own men who advanced in front of others. The aeroplane in charge by a mechanic Corpl LIEUT. TEICHMANN an officer; the pilot was not hurt, damaged the radiator, petrol tank & fuselage being holed; rifle were photographic apparatus, one tank, one bomb, one automatic pistol, several A machine gun and a Box of ammunition, maps before the aeroplane caught fire.	

Army Form C. 2118.

WAR DIARY
or
INTELLIGENCE SUMMARY
(Erase heading not required.)

Instructions regarding War Diaries and Intelligence Summaries are contained in F. S. Regs., Part II. and the Staff Manual respectively. Title pages will be prepared in manuscript.

Hour, Date, Place	Summary of Events and Information	Remarks and references to Appendices
L'ESTRADE 13-9-15 4.0 p.m.	Col. BRUCE SKINNER. AMS, DDMS 3rd Corps visited the field and asked the C.O. that in orders that he greatly appreciated the work done and progress shown by the 82nd Field Ambulance during their stay in the 3rd Corps, this being in view of a probable move tomorrow. F.R.D.	
14-9-15 10.0 A.M.	Orders received from ADMS to hand over the Farm at L'ESTRADE & the Dressing & advanced Dressing Station to the 70th Field Ambulance and all equipment etc thereof not allowed to indulge in Stn Talbot Shelld Stretcher Cages, Trench Stretchers.	
12.0 noon	Major HENDERSON arrive and are billeted in a field 200 yds South of L'ESTRADE. Contd	

Army Form C. 2118.

WAR DIARY
or
INTELLIGENCE SUMMARY

(Erase heading not required.)

Instructions regarding War Diaries and Intelligence Summaries are contained in F. S. Regs., Part II. and the Staff Manual respectively. Title pages will be prepared in manuscript.

Hour, Date, Place	Summary of Events and Information	Remarks and references to Appendices
L'ESTRADE 14-9-15	Orders received for the unit to move L'ESTRADE at 3.0 p.m on the 15th. Election to return by 10.0 A.M on that day.	
15-9-15 9.30AM	C Section arrive	
2.45 p.m	LIEUT. BORLAND with an advance billeting party and all motor transport leave; LIEUT. BORLAND to report to Byde Staff Captain at STRAZEELE Station at 4.0 p.m. a guide to be left at VIEUX BERQUIN.	
3.0 p.m	Unit leaves L'ESTRADE keeps one horsed ambulance wagon detailed to be at forked road at MENEGATE sheet 36 B.19.a.2.1 at 6.15 p.m to meet 1st and 2nd D.C.L.I. who would come from ERQUINGHEM. Route to Steenwerck — LE VERRIER Carrefour — VIEUX BERQUIN.	

WAR DIARY or INTELLIGENCE SUMMARY

Army Form C. 2118.

Hour, Date, Place	Summary of Events and Information	Remarks and references to Appendices
15-9-15.	An involuntary halt took place just before arriving at STEENWERCK. The 2nd horse ambulance wagon getting ditched at the nearest of horse flying over large Steam traction engine when occupied the crown of the road. B Section were marched back and after the horses had been unhooked, the wagon pulled the wagon and easily with drag ropes, no damage being done. Left at 3.30 p.m. + ten minute halt took place 1½ miles East of STEENWERCK at 4.20 p.m. LE VERRIER was passed and at 4.50 a ten minute halt took place at right angled turn about ½ way between LE VERRIER & VIEUX BERQUIN. Which latter place we reached at 5.45 p.m. and we guide Corpl BURVILL picked up, he showed us the way to our billet at a farm (MOLLEGHEM) just South of the O in Petit SEC BOIS. (Ref Map of BELGIUM 1/100,000 HAZEBROUCK 5A.) Time of Arrival 6.40 p.m. Horse Ambulance wagon with subaltern arrived at 1.0 A.M. the 16th. G.T.W.	

WAR DIARY or INTELLIGENCE SUMMARY

Army Form C. 2118.

(Erase heading not required.)

Instructions regarding War Diaries and Intelligence Summaries are contained in F. S. Regs., Part II. and the Staff Manual respectively. Title pages will be prepared in manuscript.

Hour, Date, Place	Summary of Events and Information	Remarks and references to Appendices
FERME MOLLEGHEM PETIT SEC BOIS 16-9-15		
6.0 AM	LIEUT & QM. G.W. HARRIS arrived back being treated STEENWERCK STATION, owing to an operation on a cyst this week he had had over 2 weeks sick leave by a Medical Board.	
10.0 AM	ADMS & DADMS visit camp. C.O. visits R2 and R3 per Head Quarters and finds and billets of the 5- Battalions. A foot inspection showed a few cases of slightly blistered feet. F.T.R.	
17-9-15	Weather fine and hot. A list of names of two officers & 5- other ranks was recommended for good & meritorious service in the fighting round YPRES during period April 28nd/15 — May 29th/15 - Thursday, Capt. A...	

Army Form C. 2118.

WAR DIARY
or
INTELLIGENCE SUMMARY
(Erase heading not required.)

Hour, Date, Place	Summary of Events and Information	Remarks and references to Appendices
FERME MOLLEGHEM PETIT SEC BOIS		
14-9-15	Contd. — being in addition to following names already in names:	
	Cpl H.S. HOLLIS RAMC (TF)	
	Pte MARTIN RAMC (TF)	
	Pte MORGAN. A Sc. MT. att d.	
	Pte JACOBS RAMC (TF)	
	He did service by C.O. as follows:	
	LIEUT & QM. G.W. HARRIS RAMC (TF)	
	LIEUT. J.W. CAIRNS RAMC (TF)	
	020466 Corpl. GREENWOOD. J. A Sc. MT. att d.	
	424 SERGT. JENKINS. W.F. RAMC (TF)	
	2413 Pte ROWDEN. R RAMC (TF)	
	2458 Pte COLEMAN. E. RAMC (TF)	
	439 Sergt SHARPE. W. RAMC (TF)	
6.30pm	The 7 Motor Ambulances & Motor cycle sent to o/c Mot. Ambg	J.W.
	at VIEUX BERQUIN.	

Army Form C. 2118.

WAR DIARY
or
INTELLIGENCE SUMMARY
(Erase heading not required.)

Instructions regarding War Diaries and Intelligence Summaries are contained in F. S. Regs, Part II. and the Staff Manual respectively. Title pages will be prepared in manuscript.

Hour, Date, Place	Summary of Events and Information	Remarks and references to Appendices
FERME MOLLEGHEM PETIT SEC BOIS		
18-9-15 1.0 pm	Orders received from ADMS for the unit to leave	
11.0 AM	leave at 1.0 p.m on 19th and march to THIENNES, Entrain and be at railway station there by 5.28 AM on the 20th to entrain.	G.D.W.
19-9-15 1.0 pm	Unit leaves FERME MOLLEGHEM.	
5.0 pm	arrive THIENNES & bivouac.	G.D.W.
20-9-15 5.0 AM	Start loading transport on train	
8.25 AM	Train starts, with 4 ambulances & Divisional ammunition Col'n. orders to detrain at GUILLAUCOURT.	
4.30 - 5.20 pm	Halt at ABBEVILLE. water & feed horses. Cooking water provided for men.	
6-15 p m	arrive GUILLAUCOURT & detrain.	Carlyl.

Army Form C. 2118.

WAR DIARY
— or —
INTELLIGENCE SUMMARY
(Erase heading not required.)

Instructions regarding War Diaries and Intelligence Summaries are contained in F.S. Regs., Part II. and the Staff Manual respectively. Title pages will be prepared in manuscript.

Hour, Date, Place	Summary of Events and Information	Remarks and references to Appendices
20-9-15. contd. 8.0 p.	DADMS arrives and takes Co. in car to MORCOURT passing thro' BAYONVILLERS, and returns visiting the Units on mile from the Station. Visited and Capt. H.S. HOLLIS with 20 men of the heavy sector are taken on 3 cars by the DADMS to staff advanced Dressing Station at CHUIGNES taking with them rations and a good supply of dressings.	
9.0 – 10.30 p.m.	The Field Ambulance proceeds to MORCOURT and bivouac in a field on south bank of the SOMME. A very clear moonlight night.	G.T.W

WAR DIARY
or
INTELLIGENCE SUMMARY

Army Form C. 2118.

Hour, Date, Place	Summary of Events and Information	Remarks and references to Appendices
MORCOURT 21-9-15. 9.45 AM	ADMS visit Encampment and orders field ambulance to proceed to CHIGNOLLES and form dressing station there in the school.	
	Captn H.B. HOLLIS on arriving at CHUIGNES finds Captn K.P. MACKENZIE there being relieved from medical charge of 2nd D.C.L.I by return of Captn H.G. MONTEITH. D.S.O. RAME	
10.45 AM	Ghd leaves MORCOURT & passing thro' MERICOURT arrived CHIGNOLLES at 12-15 p.m. meeting on the way the 413 Regt of French Infantry.	
CHIGNOLLES 4.10 p.m	ADMS takes C.O. in his car to unload adrenal present station at CHUIGNES	
6.30 pm	C.O. visit 82nd Bgde Headquarters at CAPPY and learn disposition of troops the Regt 2nd Rgv transferred, representing the Bgde in trenches as far.	T.W.

WAR DIARY
or
INTELLIGENCE SUMMARY

(Erase heading not required.)

Army Form C. 2118.

Hour, Date, Place	Summary of Events and Information	Remarks and references to Appendices
CHIGNOLLES 22-9-15	Unit employed in clearing Schools & barns. Yesterday Rev Gilbert, in the village J.T.B. The Rev. A.T. CAPES Wesleyan Chap. attached returned.	
23-9-15	Work proceeds and Cellars & Shelters inspected and men warned for occupation by latter in case of shelling. Service in Cave (Wesleyan) given by Rev. GILBERT C.F. C.S.E 22nd Division & J.T.W.	
24-9-15	Heavy rain during the night. Entraining.	
10.45pm	Orders from ADMS to Unit & be ready to move into PROYART before noon to morrow. C.T.W.	
25-9-15 8.30AM	ADMS arrives & takes C.O. in his car to clear dressing Stn & billets at PROYART.	
1030 AM	C.O. returns and unit marches direct to PROYART. Sections & transport Moving out while crossing 30 yds of road on the ridge exposed to Emmerine view. A section of 69 th Inf Amb. 22nd Div is found at PROYART. Contd.	

WAR DIARY
or
INTELLIGENCE SUMMARY

Army Form C. 2118.

Hour, Date, Place	Summary of Events and Information	Remarks and references to Appendices
PROI ART. 25-9-15 Contd	Dressing Station is formed at ECOLE and MAIRIE. Instructions given to rates & their transport at farm. Each side of street immediately north of the church; the men billeted in former Infirmary just South of the church; the officers in a red brick building west of the church; all the buildings being close together. Two large underground shelters, occupied by the French infested and allotted(?); the one to back of Hospital for patients and orderlies, the one in front of house billets to the remainder of unit, the transport having a cellar sufficiently large at their farm. S.T.W.	
2.0 pm	Capt. H.S. HOLLIS with orders from C.O. returns from CHUIGNES leaving Capt. K.P. MACKENZIE, Sgt. INGLETON & 9 men as Staff of Advanced Dressing Station. S.T.W.	

Army Form C. 2118.

WAR DIARY
INTELLIGENCE SUMMARY
(Erase heading not required.)

Hour, Date, Place	Summary of Events and Information	Remarks and references to Appendices
PROYART. 26-9-15.	C.O. sends in the following list of names for form and inattention service during the period May 28/15 — Sept 18/15. Capt. H.S. HOLLIS (RAMC(TF)) Field & Quartermaster Act Sergt Major: G.W. HARRIS (RAMC(TF)) CLENSHAW. W.A. (RAMC) 2649 Pte. EELES. S.J. RAMC (TF) 2940 Pte. FIELDER. H.J. " " 1484 Sergt. SHELDON. C. " " 2612 Sergt. FINN. C. " " 6.0 p.m. C.O. visit ADMS and MERICOURT and make arrangement for shortly baths.	G.T.W.

Army Form C. 2118.

WAR DIARY
INTELLIGENCE SUMMARY
(Erase heading not required.)

Hour, Date, Place	Summary of Events and Information	Remarks and references to Appendices
PROYART. 27-9-15 2.0 pm	Baths started in house fitted by the French for cold douches. 3 Cauldrons found here and a few tubs. ADMS sends them. Making number up to 18. Water drawn from 2 wells in gardens at back of premises. Captain STEVENSON, RAMC, Commanding, with 3 Officers and 22 men of 78th Field Ambulance arrive for instruction for a few days; 2 Officers on h.c.o and 6 men sent to advanced Dressing Stn. G.T.W.	
28-9-15. 3.0 pm	Capt. STEVENSON returns & two wind and sends two other Officers who relieve the first two at advanced Dressing Stn. They returning tomorrow with their Quartermaster. G.T.W.	

WAR DIARY

INTELLIGENCE SUMMARY

(Erase heading not required.)

Army Form C. 2118.

Hour, Date, Place	Summary of Events and Information	Remarks and references to Appendices
PROYART. 29-9-15.	Baths are working regularly and two companies bathed per day. Water drawn from well is pumped by a manual engine to storage barrels, heated in Y Cauldrons and 24 tubs used at a time.	
3.0 p.m.	C.O. with Capt. P. WOOD visits advanced dressing station.	
30-9-15. 10.0 AM	2 Officers + 15 men of 78th Field Ambulance arrive. Change with the present party who return to their units. ADMS & DADMS arrive & inspect baths, transport and horses.	

F.T. William. Major.
Of 2nd Field Ambulance.

121/7570

Army

27 R.J. Swain

82nd Field Ambulance.

Dec. 1915

Vol VIII

Oct 1915

Army Form C. 2118

WAR DIARY
INTELLIGENCE SUMMARY
(Erase heading not required.)

Instructions regarding War Diaries and Intelligence Summaries are contained in F.S. Regs., Part II. and the Staff Manual respectively. Title pages will be prepared in manuscript.

Hour, Date, Place	Summary of Events and Information	Remarks and references to Appendices
PROYART.		
1-10-15. 1.30 pm	2nd D.C.L.I. march in after their tour of in the trenches; the last few days having been wet they bring a good deal of mud with them; 4 cases of "trench feet" not severe. They found the baths very acceptable.	G.T.N.
2-10-15. 9.30 AM	Sergt GREEN and Private HUGHES & BAMPTON proceed to BOVES to superintend the loading of underclothing in barium laundries there; Pte BAMPTON to act as interpreter. Clothes from the baths to be collected 3 times a week and sent AMERICOURT for disinfection and from there to BOVES.	
11.30 AM	ADMS visits baths & inspects some cases of "trench feet" at D.C.L.I. medical inspection room.	G.T.N.

Army Form C. 2118.

WAR DIARY
or
INTELLIGENCE SUMMARY

(Erase heading not required.)

Instructions regarding War Diaries and Intelligence Summaries are contained in F. S. Regs., Part II. and the Staff Manual respectively. Title pages will be prepared in manuscript.

Hour, Date, Place	Summary of Events and Information	Remarks and references to Appendices
PROYART.		
3-10-15.		
9-15 am	Divine Service in conjunction with 2nd Devs held by Rev. E. GILBERT.	
10.30 AM	DADMS with C.O. rode to CHUIGNES inspected advanced dressing station, and then proceeded on foot to FONTAINE-LES-CAPPY and visited the Regimental aid Post of the Royal Leicestershires and 1st Cambridge Reg.	
2.30 pm	C.O. with Capt. H.S. HOLLIS rode to Canal Bridge at FROISSY and inspected Barge 140 fitted up with 30 beds for the use of 27th Division. G.F.W.	
4-10-15.	The 82nd Light Brigade are relieved at the front line by the 83rd Light Brigade. Capt. K.P. MACKENZIE and detachments are withdrawn. Con't	

Army Form C. 2118

WAR DIARY
INTELLIGENCE SUMMARY
(Erase heading not required.)

Instructions regarding War Diaries and Intelligence Summaries are contained in F.S. Regs., Part II. and the Staff Manual respectively. Title pages will be prepared in manuscript.

Hour, Date, Place	Summary of Events and Information	Remarks and references to Appendices
PROYART. 4-10-15 Sunday	— from CHUIGNES handing over to detachment of 81st Field Ambulance at 10.0 A.M.	
9.30AM	C.O. with LIEUT. G. COCK proceed to WARFUSÉE ABANCOURT, away fr the battle to the Dressing Station and take over there from Capt. C.E. GREEN and men of F/1/1st Lanc.	
2.0 pm	Capt. H.S. HOLLIS with Sergt JENKINS and 6 men with necessary Equipment proceed to WARFUSÉE to staff the Dressing Station taking motor ambulance. The disposition of the 8 and Infanty Brigade this morning is as follows:— Head Quarters and Royal Irish Fusileers at PROYART Royal Irish Regt & 1st Cambridge Rgt at MORCOURT 2nd D.C.L.I. & 1st Leinsters at WARFUSÉE ABANCOURT.	

G.K.W.

Army Form C. 2118.

WAR DIARY
or
INTELLIGENCE SUMMARY

(Erase heading not required.)

Instructions regarding War Diaries and Intelligence Summaries are contained in F. S. Regs., Part II. and the Staff Manual respectively. Title pages will be prepared in manuscript.

Hour, Date, Place		Summary of Events and Information	Remarks and references to Appendices
PROYART. 5-10-15.	10.0 AM	The 82nd J. Bgde being out of the trenches the N.C.O. and men, attached for instruction from the 78th Field Ambulance are taken by Captain K.P. MACKENZIE to CHUIGNES and shown over the Advanced Dressing Station there and then on to the Regimental Aid Posts at FONTAINE-LES-CAPPY and the trenches; the methods of evacuating patients by day and night explained to them. G.F.W.	
6-10-15.	10.30 AM	C.O. rides to WARFUSÉE and inspects Dressing Station there; & arranges to increase staff by 4 more men; these with one horse ambulance wagon and Capt H.S. HOLLIS horse & batman are sent over in the afternoon.	
	5.30 p.m.	N.C.O. and men of 78th Field Ambulance leave to rejoin their unit. G.F.W.	

Army Form C. 2118.

WAR DIARY
INTELLIGENCE SUMMARY
(Erase heading not required.)

Instructions regarding War Diaries and Intelligence Summaries are contained in F. S. Regs., Part II. and the Staff Manual respectively. Title pages will be prepared in manuscript.

Hour, Date, Place	Summary of Events and Information	Remarks and references to Appendices
PROYART. 4-10-15.	Captain. SCROGGIE. RAMC(TF) is appointed Sanitary Officer for the Commune of PROYART. The Baths working from 8.20 AM to dark bathe 3 companies of the 1st Argyll and Sutherland Highlanders. G.T.R.	
8-10-15.	Telegram from D.D.M.S. ROUEN received stating that Pte DUNCOMBE of this unit had been diagnosed as suffering from Cerebro. Spinal Meningitis; Strict precautions taken & contacts medically examined daily; the mobile (Bacteriological) Laboratory's help asked for and also a supply of anti meningococcic serum applied for thro' ADMS. G.T.R.	

WAR DIARY
INTELLIGENCE SUMMARY
(Erase heading not required.)

Army Form C. 2118.

Hour, Date, Place	Summary of Events and Information	Remarks and references to Appendices
PROYART. 9-10-15. 12.45p.	DDMS. 12th Corps with Lt.Col. Brackenridge and ADMS & DADMS 27th Division inspects the Field Ambulances, expresses himself pleased with everything and considered the Unit the best Field Ambulance in the Corps.	
2.20pm	C.O. rides to WARFUSÉE to inspect Latrents for evacuation from Dressing Station. O/c Mobile Laboratory visits and takes contents of the care of E.S. Fever and takes swabs which proved negative.	G.T.W.
10-10-15.	C.O. is gazetted temporary Lieut. Colonel from September 19th 1915; and is granted leave from 11th — 18th October.	G.T.W.

Army Form C. 2118.

WAR DIARY

82nd Field Ambulance (2ette F'AMR. LAMOTTE)

INTELLIGENCE SUMMARY

(Erase heading not required.)

Hour, Date, Place	Summary of Events and Information	Remarks and references to Appendices
PROYART 11-10-15.	Capt. H.S. HOLLIS leaves Dressing Station at LAMOTTE, and takes over command of Unit. Capt. K.P. MACKENZIE taking his place at LAMOTTE. Capt. D.M. BORLAND proceeds to United Kingdom for 14 days leave. HSH.	
12-10-15.	Capt.s H.S. HOLLIS & J.W. CAIRNS visit CAPPY that make arrangements for taking over the advanced Dressing Station there from 83rd Field Ambulance. HSH.	
13-10-15. 4.0-9.30 pm	Captains J.W. CAIRNS & F. SCROGGIE visit the aid post of left sector of the line. HSH.	
14-10-15.	Capts. H.S. HOLLIS & P. WOOD visit ye 83rd Field Ambulance re taking over Advanced Dressing Station at CAPPY. HSH.	

Army Form C. 2118.

WAR DIARY
INTELLIGENCE SUMMARY
(Erase heading not required.)

Instructions regarding War Diaries and Intelligence Summaries are contained in F. S. Regs., Part II. and the Staff Manual respectively. Title pages will be prepared in manuscript.

Hour, Date, Place	Summary of Events and Information	Remarks and references to Appendices
PROYART. 15-10-15.	Capt. H.S. HOLLIS inspected sanitary arrangements of 82nd Infy Brigade.	ASH.
16-10-15.	Staff Sergeant C. PARRY being time expired and Qr/Sergt MANNING. A.S.C. being supernumerary same unit for the rate.	HSH.
17-10-15.	Capt. J.W. CAIRNS and C Section with 3 motor ambulances & water cart take over advanced dressing station at CAPPY from F3rd Fd. Ambulance. Capt. K.P. MacKENZIE & Lieut G. COCK with detachment return from LAMOTTE handing over to detachment of 83rd F.A. Ambulance.	
18-10-15.	Col. LIDDLE, A.S.C. inspect the Horse Transport, H.S.H. 6 sick men of the French Engineers conveyed this Field ambulance to their hospital at AMIENS. H.S. Hollis Capt RAMC T.F.	

Army Form C. 2118.

WAR DIARY
or
INTELLIGENCE SUMMARY

(Erase heading not required.)

Instructions regarding War Diaries and Intelligence Summaries are contained in F. S. Regs., Part II. and the Staff Manual respectively. Title pages will be prepared in manuscript.

Hour, Date, Place	Summary of Events and Information	Remarks and references to Appendices
PROYART		
19-10-15.		
8.30 AM	LIEUT. COL. G.T. WILLAN returns from leave and resumes command.	G.T.W.
10.30 AM	A.D.M.S. visits PROYART.	
	Capt. P. WOOD is detailed to take command of advanced Dressing Station at CAPPY vice Capt. J.W. CAIRNS who returns to PROYART for duty.	
20-10-15.	LIEUT. K. SONNTAG is detailed for temp. duty as M.O. 1/c 1st Bgde R.F.A. A.D.M.S. visits PROYART.	G.T.W.
21-10-15.		
2.0 pm	C.O. visits advanced Dressing Station at CAPPY. 80th J. Bgde relieves 82nd Bgde in left Sector of line.	
10.0 pm	Orders to hand over adv. Dressing Stn. to 83rd Fd. Ambulance on 22nd.	G.T.W.

Army Form C. 2118.

WAR DIARY
INTELLIGENCE SUMMARY
(Erase heading not required.)

Instructions regarding War Diaries and Intelligence Summaries are contained in F. S. Regs., Part II. and the Staff Manual respectively. Title pages will be prepared in manuscript.

Hour, Date, Place	Summary of Events and Information	Remarks and references to Appendices
PROYART. 22-10-15. 3.0pm	C.O. visits ADMS and inspects 2 farms on the AMIENS-PERONNE Road just East of the valley running South from MORCOURT; with orders to march from PROYART by 9.0 AM the 23rd and ready the two farms till morning of the 24th & from then to march under orders of the G.O.C. 82nd Bgde.	
5.0 pm	C Section returns to PROYART. Orders given to the field ambulance to parade in heavy order at 8.30 AM the 23rd.	

G.T.W.

WAR DIARY
or
INTELLIGENCE SUMMARY

(Erase heading not required.)

Army Form C. 2118.

Hour, Date, Place	Summary of Events and Information	Remarks and references to Appendices
PROYART.		
23-10-15. 8.5 AM	Unit leaves PROYART.	
10.0 AM	Arrives at the two Farms on AMIENS—PERONNE Road. A,B,C,C & Motor Ambulances occupy first Farm. B Sec and Horse transport Third area the farm at the dip in the road. The 5th and 119th Regts of French Infantry passed to take over.	
24-10-15	Under orders from 82nd Bgde, the 3 horsed Ambulances are detailed to be at the Flatiground – the Cross Roads West of Church in WARFUSEE-ABANCOURT at 11.25 AM under command of Capt. A.F. SCROGGIE to march in rear of 2nd D.C.L.I. 27th Division Operation Order No 67 of Oct. 22nd (S) states the horse to the horse area is to be treated by all units as a training in march discipline. Intervals of 15	Ref. Sketch 12 × 21 Ref. Maps Sheet 12 × 21 50,000 Cont.d

WAR DIARY

~~INTELLIGENCE~~ SUMMARY

(Erase heading not required.)

Army Form C. 2118.

Hour, Date, Place	Summary of Events and Information	Remarks and references to Appendices
24-10-15 Cont^d	minutes between Battalions, 3-minutes between companies and ten yards between platoons will be kept by the Infantry. Corresponding intervals will be kept in the other formations." This being the case the Field Ambulance marched as a company with 10yds between Sections and 5-minutes between the transport and rear Section'. The Triton Ambulance under command of Captⁿ N.P. MACKENZIE were ordered to start at 3.30 p.m with the view of arriving at Camp at BOVES about 5.0 p.m.	
10.45 A.M.	Unit Leaves.	
11.40 A.M.	Passes Starting Point; and marched with hourly halt of 10 minutes via VILLERS BRETONNEAUX - Point 49 - St Nicholas - BOVES.	

F. 15th Reserve. BOVES and camp in tents at Bivouacs. G.T.W.

Army Form C. 2118.

WAR DIARY
or
INTELLIGENCE SUMMARY

(Erase heading not required.)

Instructions regarding War Diaries and Intelligence Summaries are contained in F. S. Regs., Part II. and the Staff Manual respectively. Title pages will be prepared in manuscript.

Hour, Date, Place	Summary of Events and Information	Remarks and references to Appendices
Methuret. 25-10-15.	After a very wet night the Stubblefield forming the Camping Ground made it difficult to get horses on to the road. Starting Point — forked road west end of BOYES. A Sec horse ambulance detailed to be there at 9-15 AM to march behind Brigade H.Q. in centre of Column. B & C Sec. horse ambulances to leave Starting Point at 10-15 AM & march behind 1st Leinster Regt.	
10.20 AM	Unit passes Starting Point and marches via Pt FUSCIEN — DURY — SALEUX and then to Gillettrip area at FLUY	
4.0 p.m.	Arrive FLUY. 22 patients sent from Div. Rest Station at MORCOURT Cont d. —	

WAR DIARY
or
INTELLIGENCE SUMMARY

(Erase heading not required.)

Army Form C. 2118.

Hour, Date, Place	Summary of Events and Information	Remarks and references to Appendices
On the march. 25-10-15. Contd.	arrive in Cars of 81st Field Ambulance for dispersal. 3 of them only belong to 82nd Brigade. Lieut. SONNTAG leaves unit to take over duties of M.O. 1/2nd DCLI. Capt. G. COCK " " " " " " " " " " " 1st Leinsters.	
26-10-15.	Who had accompanied 82nd Bgde via Pt Cauls. The P.P.C.L.I. having arrived at their destination. FERRIERES are right; 3 horsed Ambulances and one motor ambulance are directed off & ordered to proceed at rear of Brk battalion in front their destination and return than to FRESNOY	G.T.O.
10-10 AM	Unit leaves FLUY.	
10-35 AM	Passes starting point at Cross Rds 500 yds S.W. of REVELLES.	
11-15 AM	arrive FRESNOY and settle into new billets already arranged by Lieut. & Qr G.W. HARRIS. Capt. Q.	

WAR DIARY
INTELLIGENCE SUMMARY
(Erase heading not required.)

Army Form C. 2118.

Hour, Date, Place	Summary of Events and Information	Remarks and references to Appendices
FRESNOY. 26-10-18. cont'd.	A small hospital is prepared, in empty house for 15-20 patients, staff from A Sec.	
2-30pm	ADMS & DADMS arrive and arrange for us to open an civilian hospital to take in 70 patients from Divisional Rest Station on 27th; a building is selected and prepared — staffed by C Section. Officers from No 10 M.A.C on tray arranges for motor lorries to call ever afternoon to list of patients to be taken to South husband C.C.S. at AMIENS. $\overline{\text{F.T.b.}}$ the day following. Arrival of the tractors ten of footgear. Employment of shaving station newly ? instituted, our loaded. The wagons were undoubtedly over loaded.	
29-10-15. 7.0AM	CAPT. D.M. BORLAND returns from leave.	
20pm	38 patients arrive from 27th Div Rest Station. $\overline{\text{F.T.b.}}$	

Army Form C. 2118.

WAR DIARY
INTELLIGENCE SUMMARY
(Erase heading not required.)

Hour, Date, Place	Summary of Events and Information	Remarks and references to Appendices
FRESNOY 28-10-15.	Rev. GILBERT. C.F. Leave of duty with 23rd Division. Disposition of 23rd Byde Ffs in new area is as follows:- DIV. HQ and ADMS at BOVELLES 82nd Bgde HQ at BUSSY R. Irish Regt. " COURCELLES 2nd D.C.L.I. " FRESNOY 82nd Field Ambulance " " " R. Irish Fus: " MOYENCOURT. 1st LEINSTERS " FRICAMPS 1st Cambridges. " THIEULLOY 19th Bgde R.F.A. " " 98 Co ASC " " 1st Western Fd. R.E. " FRICAMPS arrangements made for Horse Ambulance to collect "sick" Gen: morning. " HERMILLY. F.T.W.	

Army Form C. 2118.

WAR DIARY
INTELLIGENCE SUMMARY
(Erase heading not required.)

Instructions regarding War Diaries and Intelligence Summaries are contained in F.S. Regs., Part II. and the Staff Manual respectively. Title pages will be prepared in manuscript.

Hour, Date, Place	Summary of Events and Information	Remarks and references to Appendices
FRESNOY.		
29-10-15. 11.0 AM	ADMS visits unit and sees patients from 27th Div¹ Rest Station; these were ordered to be returned to their units. G.T.W.	
30-10-15. 11.0 AM	C.O. & Captⁿ H.S. HOLLIS ride to THIEULLOY & HERMILLY and arrange for the Sn O/c 1st Cambridge Reg¹ at the former place to see the daily sick of the 1st Wessex. R.E.	
2.45 pm	ADMS inspects at our hospital about 45 men of the 82nd L/¹ Boyle who were reported unfit for active service. 18 were marked A. and 6 B. G.T.W.	
31-10-15. 9.0 AM	Church Parade for Wesleyans by Rev. C.F. CAPE. C.F.	
11.0 AM	" " C of E " Rev. MACE. C.F.	
6.30 PM	" " " " Rev. CAPE. C.F.	
	Captⁿ BORLAND detailed for C of E duty with 1st Leinsters vice Captⁿ G. COCK invalided to Rouen.	

G.T. Willan Lt Col.
o/c 82nd Field Ambulance.

F/119/11/7

24th Dec.

Portion of a War Diary for ? 30.11.15.
82nd Fd. Amb.

11-14 Dec. 1915
Vol VIII

27

802nd Fr. Amb.
Nov.
Vol XI

21/11/05
F/1771/

WENT TO
SALONIKA

Nov 1915

WAR DIARY 82nd Field Ambulance.
or
~~INTELLIGENCE SUMMARY~~ 1/2nd H.C. Field and
(Erase heading not required.)   RAMC (TF)

Army Form C. 2118.

Hour, Date, Place	Summary of Events and Information	Remarks and references to Appendices
FRESNOY-AU-VAL Nov. 1st/15.	CAPT. M.H.S. HOLLIS proceeds on leave to the United Kingdom, his leave having been inaccurately held up.	
3.0 pm	ADMS inspects further "Unfits" of 2nd Bgde.	
	Capt. D.M. BORLAND detailed for temporary duty with 1st Leinster Regt at FRICAMPS during absence the same of Capt. G. COCK.	G.T.W.
2-11-15.	CAPT. P. WOOD proceeds on leave to United Kingdom.	G.T.W.
3-11-15.	Capt. J. Anstruther SMITH. RAMC(TC) and Lieut D.V. MAXWELL-ADAMS RAMC (Reserve of Officers) report for duty.	G.T.W.
4-11-15.	Capt. J.A. SMITH proceeds on short leave to United Kingdom.	G.T.W.
5-11-15.	Orders received to reorganise unit to comply with "Special Establishment for SALONIKA FORCE".	cont'd

Army Form C. 2118.

WAR DIARY
or
INTELLIGENCE SUMMARY
(Erase heading not required.)

Hour, Date, Place	Summary of Events and Information	Remarks and references to Appendices
FRESNOY.		
5-11-15 cont^d 2.30 pm	Indented Nov. 1st 1915. 31 H.D horses given up to o/c 95 Co A.S.C at BOVELLES. To be replaced by mules. 13 A.S.C. men are also taken away. Capt. St J. D. BUXTON. R.A.M.C (T.C) arrives for duty. Supernumerary. G.F.B.	
6-11-15	The Rev. F. Rusher. C.F. Roman Catholic Chaplain to the 82nd Inf^y Brigade arrived and is attached to this Field Ambulance. G.F.B.	
7-11-15	Very bad & impossible to hold the outdoor Church Service. 3 Motor Ambulances conveyed 22 men of the 2nd Bde to BOVELLES to be confirmed by the Bishop of Khartoum (Chaplain General to the Forces) G.F.B.	

Army Form C. 2118.

WAR DIARY
INTELLIGENCE SUMMARY

(Erase heading not required.)

Instructions regarding War Diaries and Intelligence Summaries are contained in F. S. Regs., Part II. and the Staff Manual respectively. Title pages will be prepared in manuscript.

Hour, Date, Place	Summary of Events and Information	Remarks and references to Appendices
FRESNOY 8-11-15.	Capt. K.R. MACKENZIE. Obtains permission from H.Q. 10th Corps to proceed to PARIS for 24 hours leave. Lieut. D.V. MAXWELL-ADAMS proceeds to TREPORT on 24 hours leave.	G.T.W.
9-11-15.	Sergt F. DICKENSON. A.S.C. M.T. leaves the unit and proceeds to ENGLAND on being promoted to Staff Sergeant.	G.T.W.
10-11-15.	Capt. P. WOOD returns from leave.	G.T.W.
11-11-15.	Remaining Horses of the unit handed over to 95 Co. A.S.C. at BOVELLES and replaced by Mules; owing to Light Ambulance wagons not being available 10 teams of Pair mules are arranged for. 42 men of A.S.C. from 25 Res. S.A.A. Park are also taken over.	G.T.W.

Army Form C. 2118.

WAR DIARY
INTELLIGENCE SUMMARY
(Erase heading not required.)

Instructions regarding War Diaries and Intelligence Summaries are contained in F. S. Regs., Part II. and the Staff Manual respectively. Title pages will be prepared in manuscript.

Hour, Date, Place	Summary of Events and Information	Remarks and references to Appendices
FRESNOY. 12-11-15.	Very wet. C.O. visits ADMS at BOVELLES.	G.T.D.
13-11-15.	2/LIEUT. A.P. DAVIES A.S.C. has arrived to be attached to this Field Ambulance as Transport Officer.	G.T.D.
14-11-15.	Very wet morning. A Short Parade Church Service was held at 10.0 A.M. in Carpenters Loft 2nd D.C.L.I. by Rev. J.B. MACE. Afternoon fine & colder.	G.T.D.

WAR DIARY
INTELLIGENCE SUMMARY
(Erase heading not required.)

Army Form C. 2118.

Hour, Date, Place	Summary of Events and Information	Remarks and references to Appendices
FRESNOY. 15-11-15-	3 cases of Measles have occurred in the 1st/5g Royal Irish Regt. at COURCELLES and been evacuated to L'Etoile Hospital by a Section of 2w/16 M.A.C. now stationed at FLUY.	G.W.
16-11-15-	It has been decided that, in accordance with establishments for SALONIKA FORCE 1915: that the transport of Field Ambulances should be A.S.C. All the R.A.M.C. Transport are willing to remain if into the A.S.C. & those who when A.S.C. men can be obtained will be transferred from Transport into Bearer Subdivisions of the Field Ambulance.	G.W.

Army Form C. 2118.

WAR DIARY
or
INTELLIGENCE SUMMARY

(Erase heading not required.)

Hour, Date, Place	Summary of Events and Information	Remarks and references to Appendices
FRESNOY. 17-11-15.	C.O. visits COUREULES with Capt.M. H.S. HOLLIS and Lees 2 fresh cases of measles this am and to suspected cases among the contacts, in an outbuilding of the chateau there. G.T.W.	
18-11-15.	Capt. D.M. BORLAND is detailed to take medical charge of 1st Bn. Leinster Regt. at FRICAMPS Capt. G. COCK having proceeded on leave to the United Kingdom. G.T.W.	
19-11-15.	Capt. F. SCROGGIE is granted short leave to France & the United Kingdom, also the Rev. A.T. EARS. Rev. J.B. MACE; also Capt. MAGNER m/o 1/Camb, who on his return is to take up permanent duty with 1/8 Leinster Rgt. G.T.W.	

WAR DIARY

INTELLIGENCE SUMMARY

(Erase heading not required.)

Army Form C. 2118.

Hour, Date, Place	Summary of Events and Information	Remarks and references to Appendices
FRESNOY. 20-11-15.	Capt. J.T. DIXON M.O. i/c 1st Bn R.Irish Regt. is granted leave. A medical officer is detailed from the daily list from this Field Ambulance.	G.T.W.
21-11-15.	C.O. visits M.O. i/c 2nd R. Irish Fusiliers at MOYENCOURT. Capt. A. VENABLES who was ill is led. Capt. K.P. MACKENZIE is detailed to do his work temporarily.	G.T.W.
22-11-15.	Orders received from ADMS for unit to leave FRESNOY at 12.20 p.m. on 23rd and march to GUINEMICOURT arriving there by 4 p.m. Capt. F. SCROGGIE on his return detailed to accompany the 1st R. Irish Regt. on their journey & till arrival of their Mr. O., the Rev's J.B.MACE & RUSHER (Join 2nd DCLI & Leinster Regt. for the journey.	G.T.W.

Army Form C. 2118.

WAR DIARY
INTELLIGENCE SUMMARY

(Erase heading not required.)

Instructions regarding War Diaries and Intelligence Summaries are contained in F. S. Regs., Part II. and the Staff Manual respectively. Title pages will be prepared in manuscript.

Hour, Date, Place	Summary of Events and Information	Remarks and references to Appendices
FRESNOY. 23/11/15 12.30 PM.	The Field Ambulance leaves FRESNOY, and marching thro' PISSY arrive at GUIGNEMICOURT at 3.45 p.m.; & goes into billets for the night.	G.T.W.
24-11-15 11.30 AM	Unit leaves GUIGNEMICOURT and marches to LONGEAU Station arriving at 3.0 p.m., and with 23rd Fd Amb. entraining Fd Ambulance wagons, mules & riding horses there returning to camp at GUIGNEMICOURT under command of Lieut. DAVIES. A.S.C. Train started at 5.25 p.m.	G.T.W.
25-11-15	Train stops for 1 hour at MELUN (7-8 A.M.) short halts at DIJON & LYON.	G.T.W.
26-11-15	Arrive MARSEILLES, 4.30 p.m. and embark on H.M.T. SATURNIA. (Donaldson Line) as only our limbers & forge cart can be taken on board.	Cont'd

Army Form C. 2118.

WAR DIARY
INTELLIGENCE SUMMARY
(Erase heading not required.)

Instructions regarding War Diaries and Intelligence Summaries are contained in F. S. Regs., Part II. and the Staff Manual respectively. Title pages will be prepared in manuscript.

Hour, Date, Place	Summary of Events and Information	Remarks and references to Appendices
26-11-15 Cont'd	Corpl. MASKERY and 3 men are left in Charge of the 6 G.S. Wagons. G.S.W.	
H.M.T. SATURNIA. 27-11-15	Troops on Board are 2nd R. Irish Fusiliers under Lt. Col. ORPEN PALMER (O.C. TROOPS) 1 Batt. 1st Leinster Regt. under Major WILDBLOOD. 2 to Divisional Cyclists; a Field Co. R.E. 22nd Division. 21st 82nd 83rd Field Ambulances; 28 Casualty Clearing Station under Lieut Col NICKERSON. V.C. RAMC who is attd. P.M.O. MAJOR. PEYTON RAMC(TF) is appointed Sanitary Officer. Capt. D.M. BORLAND & Lieut D.V. MAXWELL-ADAMS are detailed to report to A.D.M.S. MARSEILLES for duty on other Transports. Capt. F. SCROGGIE returns to the unit on arrival & Lieut. J.T. DIXON from leave. Ship remains in harbour at Quay Side. G.S.W.	

Army Form C. 2118.

WAR DIARY
INTELLIGENCE SUMMARY
(Erase heading not required.)

Instructions regarding War Diaries and Intelligence Summaries are contained in F.S. Regs., Part II. and the Staff Manual respectively. Title pages will be prepared in manuscript.

Hour, Date, Place	Summary of Events and Information	Remarks and references to Appendices
H.M.T SATURNIA		
28-11-15 11.40AM	Ship sails and arrives TOULON harbour at 4.20 p.m. & makes fast to buoy.	
11.0 p.m.	Sails. G.F.W.	
29-11-15	Fine & Cold. Ship's Cruise is between CORSICA & ELBA. F.V.W.	
30-11-15	Slight greenness - about ⅔ the troops suffering from sea-sickness. All men wear life belts except at night when they may remove them keeping them close at hand. All troops paraded at 10.0 AM for inspection daily. Life boat & raft parties detailed. Whistle toto turn on Boat & Saloon lookoff fly seal drill.	

G.F.Willan, Lt.Col.
o/c 82nd Field Ambulance.

www.ingramcontent.com/pod-product-compliance
Lightning Source LLC
Chambersburg PA
CBHW081435160426
43193CB00013B/2283